KREGEL CLASSIC SERMONS SERIES

CLASSIC SERMONS
ON THE
WORD OF GOD

Compiled by
Warren W. Wiersbe

kregel
PUBLICATIONS

Grand Rapids, MI 49501

Classic Sermons on the Word of God
Compiled by Warren W. Wiersbe

Published by Kregel Publications, a division of Kregel, Inc., P.O. Box 2607, Grand Rapids, MI 49501. Kregel Publications provides trusted, biblical publications for Christian growth and service. Your comments and suggestions are valued.

For more information about Kregel Publications, visit our web site at http://www.kregel.com.

Cover photo: Copyright © 1997 Kregel Publications
Cover and book design: Alan G. Hartman

Library of Congress Cataloging-in-Publication Data
Classic sermons on the Word of God / Warren W. Wiersbe, compiler.
    p.   cm.— (Kregel classic sermons series)
  Includes index.
  1. Bible—Sermons. 2. Sermons, American. 3. Sermons, English—Scotland. 4. Sermons, English. I. Wiersbe, Warren W. II. Series.
BS491.5.C53   1997   252—dc21   97-27914
                                        CIP
ISBN   0-8254-4080-7

Printed in the United States of America

1 2 3 / 03 02 01 00 99 98 97

CONTENTS

LIST OF SCRIPTURE TEXTS

PREFACE

THE *KREGEL CLASSIC SERMONS SERIES* is an attempt to assemble and publish meaningful sermons from master preachers about significant themes.

These are *sermons,* not essays or chapters taken from books about themes. Not all of these sermons could be called great, but all of them are *meaningful.* They apply the truths of the Bible to the needs of the human heart, which is something that all effective preaching must do.

While some are better known than others, all of the preachers whose sermons I have selected had important ministries and were highly respected in their day. The fact that a sermon is included in this volume does not mean that either the compiler or the publisher agrees with or endorses everything that the man did, preached, or wrote. The sermon is here because it has a valued contribution to make.

These are sermons about *significant* themes. The pulpit is no place to play with trivia. The preacher has thirty minutes in which to help mend broken hearts, change defeated lives, and save lost souls; he can never accomplish this demanding ministry by distributing homiletical tidbits. In these difficult days we do not need clever pulpiteers who discuss the times; we need dedicated ambassadors who will preach the eternities.

The reading of these sermons can enrich your spiritual life. The studying of them can enrich your skills as an interpreter and expounder of God's truth. However God uses these sermons in your life and ministry, my prayer is that His church around the world will be encouraged and strengthened by them.

WARREN W. WIERSBE

The Bible Tried and Proved

Charles Haddon Spurgeon (1834–1892) is undoubtedly the most famous minister of the nineteenth century. Converted in 1850, he united with the Baptists and soon began to preach in various places. He became pastor of the Baptist church in Waterbeach, England, in 1851, and three years later he was called to the decaying Park Street Church, London. Within a short time the work began to prosper, a new church was built and dedicated in 1861, and Spurgeon became London's most popular preacher. In 1855, he began to publish his sermons weekly; today they make up the fifty-seven volumes of *The Metropolitan Tabernacle Pulpit*. He founded a pastor's college and several orphanages.

This sermon was taken from *The Metropolitan Tabernacle Pulpit,* volume 35.

Charles Haddon Spurgeon

1

THE BIBLE TRIED AND PROVED

The words of the LORD are pure words: as silver tried in a furnace of earth, purified seven times (Psalm 12:6).

IN THIS PSALM our text stands in contrast with the evil of the age. The psalmist complains that the "godly man ceaseth; the faithful fail from among the children of men." It was a great grief to him, and he found no consolation except in the words of the Lord. What if men fail—the Word of the Lord abides! What a comfort it is to quit the arena of controversy for the green pastures of revelation! One feels like Noah when, shut within the ark, he saw no longer the death and desolation that reigned outside. Live in communion with the Word of God and, in the absence of Christian friends, you will not lack for company.

Furthermore, the verse stands in fuller contrast still with the words of the ungodly when they rebel against God and oppress His people. They said, "With our tongue will we prevail; our lips are our own: who is lord over us?" They boasted, they domineered, they threatened. The psalmist turned away from the voice of the boaster to the words of the Lord. He saw the promise, the precept, and the doctrine of pure truth, and these consoled him while others spoke every man vanity with his neighbor. He had not so many of the words of the Lord as we have, but what he had made his own by meditation he prized above the finest gold. In the good company of those who had spoken under divine direction, he was able to bear the threats of those who surrounded him. So, dear friend, if at any time your lot is cast where the truths you love so well are despised, get back to the prophets and apostles and hear through them what God the Lord will speak. The voices of earth are full of falsehood, but the word from heaven is very pure. There is a good practical lesson in the position of the text, learn it well. Make the Word of God your daily companion. Then, whatever may grieve you in the false doctrine of the hour, you will not be too much cast down, for the words of the Lord will sustain your spirit.

Looking at the text, does it not strike you as a marvel of condescension that Jehovah, the infinite, should use words? He has arranged for us, in His wisdom, this way of communicating with one another. But as for Himself, He is pure spirit and boundless. Shall He contract His glorious thoughts into the narrow channel of sound, ear, and nerve? Must the eternal mind use human words? The glorious Jehovah spoke worlds. The heavens and the earth were the utterances of His lips. To Him it seems more in accordance with His nature to speak tempests and thunders, than to stoop to the humble vowels and consonants of a creature of the dust. Will He in very deed communicate with man in man's own way? Yes, He stoops to speak to us by words. We bless the Lord for verbal inspiration, of which we can say, "I have esteemed the words of thy mouth more than my necessary food."

I do not know of any other inspiration, neither am I able to conceive of any that can be of true service to us. We need a plain revelation upon which we can exercise faith. If the Lord had spoken to us by a method in which His meaning was infallible, but His words were questionable, we would have been rather puzzled than edified. For it is a task indeed to separate the true sense from the doubtful words. We would always be afraid that the prophet or apostle had not, after all, given us the divine sense. It is easy to hear and to repeat words, but it is not easy to convey the meaning of another into perfectly independent words of your own. The meaning easily evaporates. But we believe that holy men of old, though using their own language, were led by the Spirit of God to use words which were also the words of God. The divine Spirit so operated upon the spirit of the inspired writer that he wrote the words of the Lord. We, therefore, treasure up every one of them. To us "every word of God is pure," and withal full of soul nutriment. "Man doth not live by bread only, but by every word that proceedeth out of the mouth of the LORD doth man live." We can heartily declare with the psalmist, "Thou art my portion, O LORD: I have said that I would keep thy words."

Our condescending God is so well pleased to speak to us by words that He has even deigned to call His only-begotten Son the "Word": "The Word was made flesh, and dwelt among us." The Lord uses words, not with reluctance, but with pleasure. He would have us think highly of them, too, as He said to Israel by Moses, "Therefore shall ye lay up these my words in your heart and in your soul."

We believe that we have the words of God preserved for us in the Scriptures. We are exceedingly grateful that it is so. If we had not the words of the Lord thus recorded, we would have felt that we lived in an evil time, since neither voice nor oracle is heard today. I say, we would have fallen upon evil days if the words that God spoke of old had not been recorded under His superintendence. With this Book before us, what the Lord spoke two thousand years ago He virtually speaks now: "He . . . will not call back his words" (Isa. 31:2). His Word abides forever. It was spoken, not for one occasion, but for all ages. The Word of the Lord is so instinct with everlasting life and eternal freshness that it is as vocal and forceful in the heart of the saint today as it was to the ear of Abraham when he heard it in Canaan, or to the mind of Moses in the desert, or to David when he sang it to his harp. I thank God that many of us know what it is to hear the divine Word respoken in our souls! By the Holy Spirit the words of Scripture come to us with a present inspiration. Not only has the Book been inspired, *it is* inspired. This Book is more than paper and ink; it talks with us. Was not that the promise?: "When thou awakest, it shall talk with thee." We open the Book with this prayer, "Speak, Lord; for thy servant heareth." And we often close it with this feeling, "Here am I; for thou didst call me." As surely as if the promise had never been uttered before, but had been spoken out of the excellent glory for the first time, the Lord has made Holy Scripture to be His direct word to our heart and conscience. I say not this of all of you, but I can say it assuredly of many here present. May the Holy Spirit at this hour speak to you yet again!

In trying to handle my text, there will be three points to dwell upon. First, *the quality of the words of God*— "The words of the LORD are pure words." Secondly, *the trials of the words of God*—"silver tried in a furnace of earth, purified seven times." Then, thirdly, *the claims of these words* derived from their purity and the trials that they have undergone. Eternal Spirit, help me to speak correctly concerning Your own Word, and help us to feel correctly while we hear!

The Quality of the Words of God

"The words of the LORD are pure words." From this statement I gather, first, *the uniformity of their character*. No exception is made to any of the words of God, but they are all described as "pure words." They are not all of the same character. Some are for teaching, others are for comfort, and others for rebuke. But they are so far of a uniform character that they are all "pure words." I conceive it to be an evil habit to make preferences in Holy Scripture. We must preserve this volume as a whole. Those sin against Scripture who delight in doctrinal texts, but omit the consideration of practical passages. If we preach doctrine, they cry, "How sweet!" They will hear of eternal love, free grace, and the divine purpose. I am glad they will. To such I say, Eat the fat, and drink the sweet; and rejoice that there are fat things full of marrow in this Book. But remember that men of God in the old times took great delight in the commands of the Lord. They had respect to Jehovah's precepts, and they loved His law. If any turn on their heel, and refuse to hear of duties and ordinances, I fear that they do not love God's Word at all. He that does not love it all, loves it not at all. On the other hand, they are equally mistaken who delight in the preaching of duties, but care not for the doctrines of grace. They say, "That sermon was worth hearing, for it has to do with daily life." I am very glad that they are of this mind. But if, at the same time, they refuse other teaching of the Lord, they are greatly faulty. Jesus said, "He that is of God heareth God's words." I fear you are not of God if you account a portion of the Lord's words to be unworthy of your consideration.

Beloved, we prize the whole range of the words of the Lord. We do not set aside the histories any more than the promises.

> I'll read the histories of thy love,
> And keep thy laws in sight,
> While through the promises I rove
> With ever fresh delight.

Above all, do not drop into the semiblasphemy of some who think the New Testament vastly superior to the Old. I would not err by saying that in the Old Testament you have more of the bullion of truth than in the New, for therein I should be falling into the evil that I condemn. But this I will say, that they are of equal authority and cast such light upon each other that we could not spare either of them. "What therefore God hath joined together, let not man put asunder." In the whole Book, from Genesis to Revelation, the words of Jehovah are found, and they are always pure words.

Neither is it right for any to say, "Thus spoke Christ Himself; but such-and-such a teaching is Pauline." No, it is not Pauline. If it be here recorded, it is of the Holy Spirit. Whether the Holy Spirit speaks by Isaiah or Jeremiah or John or James or Paul, the authority is still the same. Even concerning Jesus Christ our Lord this is true. He says of Himself, "The word which ye hear is not mine, but the Father's which sent me." In this matter He puts Himself upon the level of others who were as the mouth of God. He says again, "For I have not spoken of myself; but the Father which sent me, he gave me a commandment, what I should say, and what I should speak." We accept the words of the apostles as the words of the Lord, remembering what John said: "We are of God: he that knoweth God heareth us; he that is not of

God heareth not us. Hereby know we the spirit of truth, and the spirit of error" (1 John 4:6). A solemn judgment is thus pronounced upon those who would set the Spirit of Jesus against the Spirit who dwelled in the apostles. The words of the Lord are not affected in their value by the medium through which they came. Revealed truth is all of the same quality, even when the portions of it are not of the same weight of metal.

Abiding by the text, we observe next *the purity of the words of the Lord:* "The words of the LORD are pure words." In commerce there is silver, and silver, as you all know: silver with alloy, and silver free from baser metal. The Word of God is the silver without the dross. It is as silver which has been purified seven times in a crucible of earth in the furnace until every worthless particle has been removed. It is absolutely pure. David said truly, "Thy word is truth."

It is truth in the form of goodness *without admixture of evil.* The commandments of the Lord are just and right. We have occasionally heard opponents carp at certain coarse expressions used in our translation of the Old Testament. But the coarseness of translators is not to be set to the account of the Holy Spirit, but to the fact that the force of the English language has changed, and modes of expression that were current at one period become too gross for another. Yet, this I will assert, that I have never yet met with a single person to whom the words of God have of themselves suggested any evil thing. I have heard a great many horrible things said, but I have never met with a case in which any man has been led into sin by a passage of Scripture. Perversions are possible and probable, but the Book itself is preeminently pure. Details are given of very gross acts of criminality, but they leave no injurious impress upon the mind. The saddest story of Holy Scripture is a beacon and never a lure. This is the cleanest, clearest, purest Book extant among men. No, it is not to be mentioned in the same hour with the fabulous records that pass for holy books. It comes from God, and every word is pure.

It is also a book pure in the sense of truth, being

without admixture of error. I do not hesitate to say that I believe that there is no mistake whatever in the original Holy Scriptures from beginning to end. There may be, and there are, mistakes of translation, for translators are not inspired. But even the historical facts are correct. Doubt has been cast upon them here and there, and at times with great show of reason—doubt which it has been impossible to meet for a season. But only give space enough, and search enough, and the stones buried in the earth cry out to confirm each letter of Scripture. Old manuscripts, coins, and inscriptions are on the side of the Book. Against it there are nothing but theories and the fact that many an event in history has no other record but that which the Book affords us. The Book has been of late in the furnace of criticism. But much of that furnace has grown cold from the fact that the criticism is beneath contempt. "The words of the LORD are pure words": there is not an error of any sort in the whole compass of them. These words come from Him who can make no mistake, and who can have no wish to deceive His creatures. If I did not believe in the infallibility of the Book, I would rather be without it. If I am to judge the Book, it is no judge of me. If I am to sift it like the heap on the threshing floor and lay *this* aside and only accept *that* according to my own judgment, then I have no guidance whatever unless I have conceit enough to trust to my own heart. The new theory denies infallibility to the words of God, but practically imputes it to the judgments of men. At least, this is all the infallibility that they can get at. I protest that I will rather risk my soul with a guide inspired from heaven, than with the differing leaders who arise from the earth at the call of "modern thought."

Again, this Book is pure in the sense of reliableness. It has in its promises *no admixture of failure.* Mark this. No prediction of Scripture has failed. No promise that God has given will turn out to be mere verbiage. "Hath he said, and shall he not do it?" Take the promise as the Lord gave it, and you will find Him faithful to every jot and tittle of it. Some of us are not yet entitled to be called "old and gray-headed," though the iron-gray is pretty conspicuous upon our heads. But hitherto we have believed the promises of God, and tested and tried them. What is our verdict? I bear my solemn testimony that I have not found one word of the Lord fall to the ground. The fulfillment of a promise has been delayed sometimes beyond the period that my impatience would have desired. But to the right instant the promise has been kept, not to the ear only, but in deed and in truth. You may lean your whole weight upon any one of the words of God, and they will bear you up. In your darkest hour you may have no candle but a single promise, and yet that lone light shall make high noon of your midnight. Glory be to His name, the words of the Lord are without evil, without error, and without failure.

Furthermore, on this first head, the text not only speaks of the uniform character of God's words and of their purity, but of *their preciousness*. David compares them to refined silver, and silver is a precious metal. In other places he has likened these words to pure gold. The words of the Lord might have seemed comparable to paper money, such as our own bank notes. But no, they are the metal itself. I recollect the time when a friend of ours used to go into the western counties, from one farm to another, buying cheese. He was in the habit of taking quite a weight of coin with him, for he found that the farmers of that period did not care for bank notes and would not look at checks. But they were more ready to sell when they saw that they would be paid in metal, down on the nail. In the words of God you have the solid money of truth. It is not fiction, but the substance of truth. God's words are as bullion. When you have them in the grip of faith, you have the substance of things hoped for. Faith finds in the promise of God the reality of what she looks for: the promise of God is as good as the performance itself. God's words—whether of doctrine, of practice, or of comfort—are of solid metal to the man of God who knows how to put them in the purse of personal faith. As we use silver in many articles within our houses, so do we use God's

Word in daily life. It has a thousand uses. As silver is current coin of the merchant, so are the promises of God a currency both for heaven and earth. We deal with God by His promises, and so He deals with us. As men and women deck themselves with silver by way of ornament, so are the words of the Lord our jewels and our glory. The promises are things of beauty which are a joy forever. When we love the Word of God, and keep it, the beauty of holiness is upon us. This is the true ornament of character and life, and we receive it as a love gift from the Bridegroom of our souls.

Beloved, I need not enlarge in your presence upon the preciousness of the Word of God. You have, many of you, prized it long and have proved its value. I have read of a German Christian woman who was accustomed to mark her Bible whenever she met with a passage that was specially precious to her. But toward the end of her life she ceased from the habit, for she said, "I find it unnecessary; for the whole of the Scripture has now become most precious to me." To some of us the priceless volume is marked from beginning to end by our experience. It is all precious, and altogether precious.

> No treasures so enrich the mind,
> Nor shall thy word be sold
> For loads of silver well refined,
> Nor heaps of choicest gold.

Furthermore, this text sets before us not only the purity and preciousness of the Lord's words, but *the permanence* of them. They are as silver that has passed through the hottest fires. Truly, the Word of God has, for ages, stood the fire—and fire applied in its fiercest form: "tried in a furnace of earth"—that is to say, in that furnace which refiners regard as their last resort. If the Devil could have destroyed the Bible, he would have brought up the hottest coals from the center of hell. He has not been able to destroy one single line. Fire, according to the text, was applied in a skillful way: silver is placed in a crucible of earth that the fire may get at it thoroughly. The refiner is quite sure to employ his heat in the best manner known to him, so as to melt away the dross. So have men with diabolical skill endeavored, by the most clever criticism, to destroy the words of God. Their object is not purification; it is the purity of Scripture that annoys them. They aim at consuming the divine testimony. Their labor is vain, for the sacred Book remains still what it always was, the pure words of the Lord. But some of our misconceptions of its meaning have happily perished in the fires.

The words of the Lord have been tried frequently, aye, they have been tried perfectly—"purified *seven* times." What more remains I cannot guess, but assuredly the processes have already been many and severe. It abides unchanged. The comfort of our fathers is our comfort. The words that cheered our youth are our support in age. "The grass withereth, the flower fadeth: but the word of our God shall stand for ever." These words of God are a firm foundation, and our eternal hopes are wisely built thereon. We cannot permit anyone to deprive us of this basis of hope. In the olden times men were burned rather than cease to read their Bibles. We endure less brutal oppositions, but they are far more subtle and difficult to resist. Still let us always abide by the everlasting words, for they will always abide by us.

Unchanged, unchangeable are the words of the Ever Blessed. They are as silver without dross, which will continue from age to age. This we do believe, and in this we do rejoice. Nor is it a tax upon our faith to believe in the permanence of Holy Scripture, for these words were spoken by Him who is Omniscient and knows everything. Therefore there can be in them no mistake. They were spoken by Him who is Omnipotent, and can do everything; and therefore his words will be carried out. Spoken by Him who is immutable, these words will never alter. The words that God spoke thousands of years ago are true at this hour, for they come from Him who is the same yesterday, today, and forever. He that spoke these words is infallible, and therefore they are infallible. When did He ever err? Could He err and yet be God? "Hath he said, and shall he not do it? or hath he spoken, and shall he not make it good?" Rest you sure of this, "The words of the LORD are pure words."

The Trials of the Words of God

They are said to be as silver that has been tried in a furnace. The words of God have been tested by blasphemy, by ridicule, by persecution, by criticism, and by candid observation. I shall not attempt an oratorical flight while describing the historical tests of the precious metal of divine revelation, but I shall mention trials of a commonplace order that have come under my own notice, and probably under yours also. This may be more homely, but it will be more edifying. The Lord help us!

In dealing with *the sinner's obstinacy,* we have tested the words of the Lord. There are men who cannot be convinced or persuaded. They doubt everything, and with closed teeth they resolve not to believe, though a man declare it to them. They are encased in the armor of prejudice and cannot be wounded with the sharpest arrows of argument, though they profess great openness to conviction. What is to be done with the numerous clan who are related to Mr. Obstinate? You might as well argue with an express train as with Mr. Obstinate. He runs on and will not stop, though a thousand should stand in his way. Will the words of God convince him? There are some in this place today of whom I should have said, if I had known them before their conversion, that it was a vain task to preach the Gospel to them. They so much loved sin and so utterly despised the things of God. Strangely enough, they were among the first to receive the Word of God when they came under the sound of it. It came to them in its native majesty, in the power of the Holy Spirit. It spoke with a commanding tone to their inmost heart. It threw open the doors that had long been shut up and rusted on their hinges, and Jesus entered to save and reign. These, who had defiantly brandished their weapons, threw them down and surrendered unconditionally to almighty love, willing believers in the Lord Jesus.

Friends, we have only to have faith in God's Word and

speak it out straight, and we shall see proud rebels yielding. No mind is so desperately set on mischief, so resolutely opposed to Christ, that it cannot be made to bow before the power of the words of God. Oh that we used more the naked sword of the Spirit! I am afraid we keep this two-edged sword in a scabbard, and somewhat pride ourselves that the sheath is so elaborately adorned. What is the use of the sheath? The sword must be made bare, and we must fight with it without attempting to garnish it. Tell forth the words of God. Omit neither the terrors of Sinai, nor the love-notes of Calvary. Proclaim the word with all fidelity, as you know it, and cry for the power of the Highest, and the most obstinate sinner out of hell can be laid low by its means. The Holy Spirit uses the Word of God. This is His one battering-ram with which he casts down the strongholds of sin and self in those human hearts with which He effectually deals. The Word of God will bear the tests furnished by the hardness of the natural heart, and it will by its operations prove its divine origin.

Here begins another trial. When you have a man fairly broken down, he has but come part of the way. A new difficulty arises. Will the words of the Lord overcome *the penitent's despair?* The man is full of terror on account of sin, and hell has begun to burn within his bosom. You may talk to him lovingly, but his soul refuses to be comforted. Until you bring the words of the Lord to bear upon him "his soul abhorreth all manner of meat." Tell him of a dying Savior; dwell on free grace and full pardon; speak of the reception of the prodigal son and of the Father's changeless love. Attended by the power of the Spirit, these truths must bring light to those who sit in darkness. The worst forms of depression are cured when Holy Scripture is believed. Often have I been baffled when laboring with a soul convinced of sin and unable to see Jesus. But I have never had a doubt that in the end the words of the Lord would become a cup of consolation to the fainting heart. We may be baffled for a season, but with the words of the Lord as our weapons, Giant Despair will not defeat us. O you that are in bondage under fear of punishment, you shall come forth to liberty yet. Your chains shall be broken if you will accept the words of God. My Master's Word is a great opener of prison doors. He has broken the gates of brass and cut the bars of iron asunder.

That must be a wonderful word that, like a battle ax, smashes in the helmet of presumption, and at the same time, like the finger of love, touches the tender wound of the bleeding and heals it in an instant. The words of the Lord, for breaking down or lifting up, are equally effectual.

In certain instances, the words of God are tried *by the seeker's singularity*. How frequently have persons told us that they were sure there was nobody like themselves in all the world! They were men up in a corner—strange fish, the like of which no sea could yield. Now, if these words be indeed of God, they will be able to touch every case—but not else. The words of God have been put to that test, and we are amazed at their universal adaptation. There is a text to meet every remarkable and out-of-the-way case. In certain instances, we have heard of an odd text concerning which we could not before see why it was written. Yet it has evidently a special fitness for a particular person to whom it has come with divine authority. The Bible may be compared to the whitesmith's bunch of keys. You handle them one by one, and say of one, "That is a strange key, surely it will fit no lock that ever was made!" But one of these days the smith is sent for to open a very peculiar lock. None of his keys touch it. At last he selects that singular specimen. See! it enters, shoots back the bolt, and gives access to the treasure. The words of this book are proved to be the words of God because they have an infinite adaptation to the varied minds that the Lord has made. What a gathering of locks we have here this morning! I could not describe you all: Bramah and Chubb, and all the rest of them, could not have devised such a variety. Yet I am sure that in this inspired volume there is a key in every way suited to each lock. Personally, when I have been in trouble, I have read the Bible until a text has seemed to stand out of the Book, and salute me, saying, "I was written specially for you." It has looked to me as if the story must have been in the mind of the writer when he penned that passage. *So it was* in the mind of that divine Author who is at the back of all these inspired pages. Thus have the words of the Lord stood the test of adaptation to the singularities of individual men.

We frequently meet with people of God who have tested the words of God in time of sore trouble. I make here an appeal to the experience of the people of God. You have lost a dear child. Was there not a word of the Lord to cheer you? You lost your property. Was there a passage in the Scriptures to meet the disaster? You have been slandered. Was there not a word to console you? You were very sick and withal depressed. Had not the Lord provided a comfort for you in that case? I will not multiply questions. The fact is that you never were high, but the Word of the Lord was up with you; you never were low, but what the Scripture was down with you. No child of God was ever in any ditch, pit, cave, or abyss but the words of God found him out. How often do the gracious promises lie in ambush to surprise us with their lovingkindness! I adore the infinity of God's goodness as I see it mirrored in the glass of Scripture.

Again, the Word of God is tried and proved as *a guide in perplexity*. Have we not been forced, at times, to come to a pause and say, "I do not know what to think about *this*. What is the proper course?" This Book is an oracle to the simple-hearted man in mental, moral, and spiritual perplexity. Oh, that we used it more! Rest assured that you never will be in a labyrinth so complicated that this Book, blessed of the Spirit, will not help you through. This is the compass for all mariners upon the sea of life: by its use you will know where lies the pole. Abide by the words of the Lord and your way will be clear.

Beloved, the words of God endure another test. They are *our preservatives in times of temptation*. You can write a book that may help a man when he is tempted in a certain direction. Will the same volume strengthen him when he is attracted in the opposite direction? Can you

conceive a book that shall be a complete ring fence, en-
circling a man in all directions? Keeping him from the
abyss yonder and from the gulf on the other side? Yet
such is this Book. The Devil himself cannot invent a
temptation which is not met in these pages. All the devils in hell together, if they were to hold parliament and
to call in the aid of all bad men, could not invent a de-
vice which is not met by this matchless library of truth.
It reaches the believer in every condition and position,
and preserves him from all evil. "Wherewithal shall a
young man cleanse his way? by taking heed thereto according to thy word."

Lastly, on this point, here is a grand test of the Book: *it
helps men to die.* Believe me, it is no child's play to die!
You and I will find ourselves in that solemn article or ever
we are aware, and then we shall need strong consolation.
Nothing upon earth ever gives me so much establishment
in the faith as to visit members of this church when they
are about to die. It is very sad to see them wasting away
or racked with pain. But, nevertheless, the chief effect
produced upon the visitor is gladsome rather than gloomy.
I have this week seen a sister well known to many of you
who has a cancer in her face, and may, in all probability,
soon be with her Lord. It is a dread affliction, and one
knows not what it may yet involve. But the gracious pa-
tient knows neither murmurs nor fears. No one in this
place, though in the flush of health, could be more calm,
more restful, than our sister is. She spoke to me with full
confidence that living or dying she is the Lord's, and she
had bright anticipations of being forever with the Lord.
The little she could say with her voice was supplemented
by a great deal, which she expressed with her eyes and
with her whole demeanor. Here was no excitement, no fa-
naticism, no action of drugs upon the brain; but a sweetly
reasonable, quiet, and assured hope of eternal joy. Beloved, it is not hard to pass out of this world when we are
resting on that old and sure Gospel that I have preached
to you these many years. Personally, I can both live and
die on the eternal truths which I have proclaimed to you.
This assurance makes me bold in preaching. Not long ago

I sat by a brother who was near his end. I said to him, "You have no fear of death?" He replied cheerfully, "I should be ashamed of myself if I had after all that I have learned of the glorious Gospel from your lips these many years. It is a joy to depart and to be with Christ, which is far better." Now, if this inspired volume with its wonderful record of the words of God helps us in the trials of life, directs us in our daily paths, and enables us to weather the last great storm, surely it is precious beyond description, "as silver tried in a furnace of earth purified seven times."

The Claims of These Words of the Lord

The claims of these words are many. First, *they deserve to be studied*. Beloved, may I urge upon you the constant searching of inspired Scripture? Here is the last new novel! What shall I do with it? Cast it on the ground. Here is another piece of fiction which has been greatly popular! What shall I do with it? Throw it on one side or thrust it between the bars of the grate. This sacred volume is the freshest of novels. It would be, to some of you, an entirely new book. We have a society for providing the Bible for readers, but we greatly need readers for the Bible. I grieve that even to some who bear the Christian name, Holy Scripture is the least read book in their library. One said of a preacher the other day, "How does he keep up the congregation? Does he always give the people something new?" "Yes," said the other, "he gives them the Gospel; and in these days, *that* is the newest thing out." It is truly so; the old, old Gospel is always new. The modern doctrine is only new in name. It is, after all, nothing but a hash of stale heresies and moldy speculations. If God has spoken, listen! If the Lord has recorded His words in a Book, search its pages with a believing heart. If you do not accept it as God's inspired word, I cannot invite you to pay any particular attention to it. But if you regard it as the Book of God, I charge you, as I shall meet you at the judgment seat of Christ, study the Bible daily. Treat not the Eternal God with disrespect, but delight in His Word.

Do you read it? Then *believe* it. Oh, for an intense belief of every word that God has spoken! Do not hold it as a dead creed, but let it hold you as with an almighty hand. Have no controversy with any one of the Lord's words. Believe without a doubt. The brother of the famous Unitarian, Dr. Priestly, was permitted to preach for his brother in his chapel in Birmingham, but he was charged to take no controversial subject. He was obedient to the letter of his instructions, but very rebellious against their spirit, seeing he took for his text, "Without controversy great is the mystery of godliness: God was manifest in the flesh." Assuredly there is no controversy among spiritual men upon the glorious truth of the incarnation of our Lord Jesus. So, also, all the words of the Lord are out of the region of debate. They are to us absolute certainties. Until a doctrine becomes an absolute certainty to a man, he will never know its sweetness. Truth has little influence upon the soul until it is fully believed.

Next, *obey the Book*. Do it freely, do it heartily, do it constantly. Err not from the commandment of God. May the Lord make you perfect in every good work, to do His will! "Whatsoever he saith unto you, do it." You that are unconverted, may you obey that Gospel word: "He that believeth and is baptized shall be saved." Repentance and faith are at once the commands and the gifts of God, neglect them not.

Furthermore, these words of God are *to be preserved*. Give up no line of God's revelation. You may not know the particular importance of the text assailed, but it is not for you to assess the proportionate value of God's words. If the Lord has spoken, be prepared to die for what He has said. I have often wondered whether, according to the notions of some people, there is any truth for which it would be worthwhile for a man to go to the stake. I should say not, for we are not sure of anything, according to the modern notion. Would it be worthwhile dying for a doctrine that may not be true next week? Fresh discoveries may show that we have been the victims of an antiquated opinion. Had we not better wait and see what will turn up? It will be a pity to be burned too soon or to lie in prison for a dogma that will, in a few years, be superseded. Beloved, we cannot endure this shifty theology. May God send us a race of men who have backbones! Men who believe something and would die for what they believe. This Book deserves the sacrifice of our all for the maintenance of every line of it.

Believing and defending the Word of God, *let us proclaim it.* Go out this afternoon, on this first Sunday of summer, and speak in the street the words of this life. Go to a cottage meeting or to a workhouse or to a lodging house and declare the divine words. "Truth is mighty, and will prevail," they say. It will not prevail if it be not made known. The Bible itself works no wonders until its truths are published abroad. Tell it out among the heathen that the Lord reigns from the tree. Tell it out among the multitude that the Son of God has come to save the lost, and that whosoever believeth in Him shall have eternal life. Make all men know that "God so loved the world, that he gave his only begotten Son, that whosoever believeth in him should not perish, but have everlasting life." This thing was not done in a corner; keep it not a secret. Go into all the world and preach the Gospel to every creature. May God bless you! Amen.

NOTES

The Harvests of the Word of God

George Campbell Morgan (1863–1945) was the son of a British Baptist preacher and preached his first sermon when he was thirteen years old. He had no formal training for the ministry, but his tireless devotion to the study of the Bible helped him to become one of the leading Bible teachers of his day. Rejected by the Methodists, he was ordained into the Congregational ministry. He was associated with Dwight L. Moody in the Northfield Bible conferences and as an itinerant Bible teacher. He is best known as the pastor of the Westminster Chapel, London (1904–1917 and 1933–1945). During his second term there, he had Dr. D. Martyn Lloyd-Jones as his associate.

Morgan published more than sixty books and booklets, and his sermons are found in *The Westminster Pulpit* (London: Hodder and Stoughton, 1906–1916). This sermon was taken from volume 9.

George Campbell Morgan

2

THE HARVESTS OF THE WORD OF GOD

> For as the rain cometh down, and the snow from heaven, and returneth not thither, but watereth the earth, and maketh it bring forth and bud, that it may give seed to the sower, and bread to the eater: so shall my word be that goeth forth out of my mouth: it shall not return unto me void, but it shall accomplish that which I please, and it shall prosper in the thing whereto I sent it (Isaiah 55:10–11).

THE FITNESS of the symbolism of this text is apparent even to the most casual observer.

Snow and rain are characterized by gentleness which merges into force. One drop of rain falls upon my hand. Brush it away, and it is not. But when the drop is multiplied and the great storm sweeps along the valley, it is almost resistless in its onrush. One feathery flake of snow falls through the atmosphere. I touch it, and it passes and is lost. Its crystal beauty destroyed forever by the rudeness of my human hand. But let that flake be multiplied and the falling snow will take hold of the thundering locomotive, clog its wheels, check its progress, bury it beneath its soft and noiseless whiteness.

Rain and snow are characterized by helplessness that grows into beneficence. We ask: "What can this drop of rain do for man? What can this flake of snow do for humanity?" And yet we know that when we pass from the individual drop to the great rain, that this in falling makes the earth laugh back in harvest and crowns the labor of the hands of humanity. There is no more exquisite word in all Scripture about nature than that simple and sublime passage: "He giveth His snow like wool." Like a warm mantle, it wraps the earth in winter time and keeps it from the penetration of more intense cold.

And so we find that rain and snow, helpless as they seem, are the very messengers of beneficence to humanity.

Again, rain and snow come to us characterized by unfruitfulness, yet generating fruitfulness wherever they fall. Life cannot be sustained by the one or the other. Neither is there in either any element of repro-ductiveness. Yet in their cooperation with the forces of "old mother earth" and with the ministries of light and air, all that is needed for life's sustenance is produced.

This is but a surface application of the truth. As we watch the rain and the snow and think upon it more care-fully, we find a most suggestive symbol of the Word of God. By the Word of God at this moment I mean all that phrase can possibly mean: the written Which reveals the Living, the Living Which seals the written; the written Which is still ours, the Living Which lies behind it and speaks through it in power to the sons of men.

This Word of God in the history of the race, what has it been? Symbols becoming substance, letters advancing to life, that which has seemed to kill becoming, presently, that which has bestowed life everywhere. In order that we may understand the value of this Word of God and learn the true method of appreciation of such value, let us take this symbolism of the prophet and consider it exactly as he has stated it: first, as to the similarities suggested; second, as to the principles revealed; and fi-nally, as to the responsibility entailed.

Let me first tabulate the phrases that we are to con-sider in this verse: "Cometh from heaven; returneth not thither; watereth the earth; maketh it bring forth, and bud; that it may give seed to the sower; and bread to the eater."

The rain and the snow come from heaven. Human beings have nothing to do with the coming of the rain and the snow. You will remember how in that great theophany of the book of Job when, after the human eloquence of his friends has providentially been silenced, God Himself begins to speak to the suffering man. He speaks to him in the midst of his sorrow and his suffering by making all His glory in creation pass before him. In the midst of that wonderful questioning of Job by God occur these two inquiries; "Hast thou entered into the treasuries of the snow?" This being translated from poetry into prose means, Do you understand the snow? Do you know from whence it comes? Can you analyze the mystery of its crystallization and deposit? Then, "Hath the rain a father?" which by some process of translation means, Are you able to generate it, to produce it? With those questions in mind, let me read again this statement of the prophet. "For as the rain cometh down and the snow from heaven." The Word of God is a message from God to humanity that humanity was unable to find out for themselves. It is never a philosophy formulated by human wisdom. It is always a revelation made, a something declared that humanity could not by searching find out. The supreme quality of the Word of God is that however men may occupy their time in discussing the methods by which we have come into possession of these documents, there is stamped upon every page of them the sign manual of Jehovah. They are great unveilings of His nature, great revelations of the deepest secrets of human life, great illumination of the problems that confront human beings by divine revelation. The Word of God is the gift of God and not the contrivance of humanity.

But it "returneth not thither." The snow and the rain pour themselves out on the face of the earth, then they melt and pass. Within a very few hours of the great rainfall, which has sweetened everything in its coming, the roads are dusty again and we say, "How soon the rain has passed." So also, soon after the snow has once come under the influence of the sun, it is gone. It has seemed to pour itself out in magnificent waste. Judged by first appearances, it seems as though this gift of heaven had been poured upon earth to be spoiled, contaminated, soiled, wasted.

So also with the Word of God. The Word of God has been given to human beings in figure and symbol, in prophecy and song, and at last in the Person of Jesus, and since He came, in exposition and explanation for centuries. Ah, me! how perpetually it seems to us as we watch the openings and processes of the decades—even of the centuries—as though this great outpouring of divine revelation was lost, falling upon humanity only to be spoiled. How often have we thought of it as wasted? No, have we not thought so of it sometimes when we have been preaching it? Have we not looked out with almost passionate desire upon audiences that have listened and passed away, apparently to frivolity and forgetfulness, and have said, "Yea, verily, as the snow and the rain from heaven, but it returneth not thither"? That is the first effect upon us after observing what happens as God gives His Word.

But there is another statement needed to complete and explain this: it "watereth the earth." Take this dust as it lies upon the highway and over the furrowed field, and know that within the dust is the making of everything that is beautiful and fruitful. But the dust does not of itself laugh in flowers; it is capable and incapable. Lying within it are all the forces of life. All the mysterious magnificence of your personality on the physical side lies within the dust at your feet, and all flowers that bloom lie there in potentiality. As the rain and snow water the earth, which is at once characterized by capacity, yet it is unable to fulfill the possibilities that lie sleeping within its own being. It makes all nature laugh with new beauty.

So also the Word of God comes to human beings in whose natures are the potentialities but not the realizations. The Word of God falls upon the centuries, upon society, upon individuals, and we thought it touched them but to be spoiled and soiled and passed. But we watched and found that by its falling the soil became productive. There is in every human being the capacity for deity. There is in every human life the potentialities of the highest and the noblest and the best. I am not discussing the question of humanity's ruin. I know the ruin; I know it in my own life. But that which is ruined is not destroyed. Without some beneficent ministry external to itself it will be destroyed. Given that ministry it is still capable of realization. The very ministry it needs is that of the Word of God. As is the rain, as is the snow to the dust, so is the Word of God to humanity in its ruin. God has not been wasting His Word. As He has given it by prophets, by seers, by psalmists, and by His Son in many a symbol and by many a sign, in many a dispensation—given it to the mocking, laughing, scoffing crowds—He knows that in all the dust that lies about Him there are potentialities. As He gives His rain and snow to smite the dust into laughter, so He has given His Word that the Word coming to human beings may touch the unrealized capacity into realization.

The prophet now adds a further truth concerning these elements in the statement, "maketh it bring forth." After the rain and the snow, the dull russet ground becomes beautiful with emerald and opal and ruby and diamond. Thus we know that when God's rain and snow touch the dust, it makes the dust bring forth.

So with the Word of God. The Word of God makes the dormant forces in man move to fulfillment. All men that have ever realized the possibilities of their own life have done so in response to some part of the Word of God, to the Word spoken, to the Word written, to the Word lived, to the revelation granted. As the snow and rain coming upon the earth make the earth answer by bringing forth, so the Word of God in the centuries, as they come and go, has provoked into realization the dormant capacities of life.

Yet another word that I have taken separately, because I think it really is separate. It is a stronger word than the former: "maketh it bring forth, and bud." I feel inclined to use here the literal Hebrew word, "and sprout." That is to say, the rain and the snow not merely touch the dust into generation but actually come again in the grass, the flowers, the fruitage. You saw that rainstorm as it swept the field yonder. You watched it come. You smiled at the helplessness of the first few drops as they fell. You were appalled at the rush of the storm as the clouds broke and swept that field. Then you watched it as the clouds passed and the sun shone. As you watched the field, it seemed as though all was lost and of no avail. You went to sleep—

and God gives to His beloved in sleep—and came back again and looked at your field. There was the sheen of the emerald all over it. First the blade and then the ear; then the full corn in the ear, and so on and on, until russet had become green and green had become golden harvest. And in that waving harvest of gold what do I find? The rain that I thought lost, the snow that I thought perished. It touched the dust with the alchemy of God, and it brought back the glorious, gracious harvest.

It is equally true that the Word of God that He has been giving for centuries has never been lost. It has come from Him to touch the failure of human life, and it has been returning to Him laughing with the harvest of ransomed souls. The Word was incarnate in the Christ supremely. And in a less and different degree but nevertheless as truly, God's Word has been reincarnate in human lives in all the passing centuries. Do not let us be afraid of the Word. I make no comparison finally between the incarnation of our blessed Lord and the incarnation of truth in the life of the believer. Nevertheless, in degree every Christian soul is a reincarnation of the Word that became incarnate in Jesus of Nazareth. Is it not so? That which is true and beautiful and of good report in you, in others, what is it but God's great Word that has touched the fiber of your being and reconstructed your broken lives to the realization of His purpose, and so to the glory of His Name. The transmuted rain makes the earth not only generate by the touch of beneficence, it makes it sprout and bud and answer back in harvest. So also, the Word reincarnate in believing souls is the harvest of the earth that supremely satisfies the heart of God.

Yet that is not all. "That it may give seed to the sower." What is this harvest for? You say for the sustenance of human life. That is not the first thing. What is the harvest for? "That it may give seed to the sower" comes before "bread to the eater." Bread to the eater is a secondary thing. Bread to the eater is provision for the toiler that he may continue his sowing and reap his harvests. But the first thing is that, in the new form in which the rain and snow return to God, there is always found the potentiality of propagation waiting for new showers and new transmutations and new harvests. This is the perpetual story of the harvests as they come and go. Always first, seed to the sower.

So with the Word of God. The Word of God taking hold of human life, changing it, becoming incarnate in it, communicates propagative power. It makes a new wealth of seed that may be scattered still further in other fields. From every life remade and sanctified by the Word of God, there must go forth the seed that will affect yet other fields and stretch out toward the consummating glory of the final harvest.

Finally we come to the last phase of the symbolism, "and bread to the eater." The issue then is also sustenance to the toiler. The one that plowed and sowed and reaped, feeds. So surely also is it with this Word of God. It becomes, as we have seen for the larger purpose, the creation of new seed that may be scattered still for the uplifting of humanity, but the Word of God is also the bread of life to the toiler. By it his own life is sustained, both in health and strength, and so he is enabled for the service for which he is created and to which he is called.

Let me pass now from these similarities to take the broader outlook and consider the great principles that are revealed.

The symbolism of this great prophetic Word teaches me, first of all, that the Word of God is purposeful. Rain and snow come certainly not for nothing and not for the display of their own wonders, but for purpose. The symbolism teaches me, second, that the Word of God is powerful. The rain and snow come to victory always; they are never defeated. And the symbolism of my text teaches me, finally, that the Word of God is prosperous. It accomplishes, it prospers, as do also rain and snow.

The Word of God is purposeful. All this is seen by the various similarities which we have rapidly surveyed. The Word of God is not given to be possessed; it is given that it may possess. The truth of God is not given that human beings may hold it. Oh, I am tired of the ones that want to know if I "hold the truth." Of course I don't "hold the truth"; no one can "hold the truth." It is too big for anyone to hold, and God has never given His Word to human beings that they may "hold the truth." The facts are truly stated in quite another way. The truth must hold the person, wrap him around, change the very fiber of his being, permeate his complete life. Unless the Word of God is doing that for me, it is failing in the first intention that God has for it. Not for our good only does it come. It is seed as well as bread. Unless we come to receive the Word as the earth takes the sun and the rain, then I am not sure that we had better not absent ourselves from every occasion when the Word is opened. If I come with my notebook to write down all I can learn about the Word of God in order that I may know it, then I am absolutely failing. But if I come to strip from my soul all the things that hide me that the Word of God may search me, if I have come to lay my life out in the light of the Word that the Word may correct it, then I shall find the Word in me is fruitful as is the snow, as is the rain upon the earth. It is a purposeful thing.

Then, thank God, it is powerful. He says it shall not return to Him void. And why not? May I not reverently say as in the presence of the inspired declaration, God's Word never returned to Him void because it never comes void from Him. Do you remember the word of the angel to the blessed Virgin? "No word of God is void." Every word of God thrills with fruitfulness. If we but know how to receive it and how to respond to it, then it shall return to Him not void but fruitful in lives changed, remolded, refashioned, sanctified.

And finally, then the Word of God is prosperous. It is so because it is His Word. "It shall not return unto me void, but it shall"—and mark the two words—"accomplish . . . prosper." The word "accomplish" means it does something, it makes something, it realizes something. The Hebrew word "prosper" literally means it "pushes forward." It is a great dynamic force. It is prosperous, moreover, by selection. "That which I please, . . . the thing whereto I sent it."

These are the principles that we must bear in mind as we take up our Bibles and come to listen to the teachings of the Word of God. It is given for a purpose; it is full of power; it accomplishes the purpose by reason of the power.

In conclusion, is it important that we inquire as to the responsibilities that are entailed? Rain and snow might fall upon the earth a long time, and there be no harvest unless the earth is prepared. The rain and snow may fall in all their prodigal munificence and magnificence upon the earth, and there will be no harvest unless the seed is sown. And rain and snow may fall and make the earth laugh with harvest if the earth be ready and the seed be sown. Yet men get no benefit unless the harvest be reaped, the seed be sown again, and through the process the bread be eaten.

Here, then, are three things at least that I would say: the earth must be prepared; take heed how you hear. The seed must be sown; preach the Word. The bread must be eaten; let the Word of Christ dwell in you richly.

Take heed how you hear. In all tenderness and yet with great earnestness and great conviction, I would sound that word in the hearing of all. Take heed how you hear. How shall we hear? Prayerfully, obediently, and in faith. The spirit of criticism never produces the result of power. Let us pray that in our lives God will plow up the fallow ground and give us receptive hearts—the child heart. May He give us a willingness to hear and learn, deliver us from preconceived notions and prejudice, make us ready when He speaks to obey, and make us simple-hearted at His feet. For as the rain and snow demand an earth plowed, broken, prepared, so does the Word of God demand a condition in those who hear, if it is to bring forth a harvest.

The true seed must be sown, and it must be by the preaching of the Word if the work is to be done. We are not to criticize the Word of God, not to account for the Word of God, not to defend the Word of God. We are to preach it and hear it. And there is a yet fuller application of that truth. The final preaching of the Word is not that of the lips but that of the life. Fundamentally the Word is the seed in the hearts of people. But functionally, for the sake of the world, the seed is the sons and daughters of the kingdom, the people in whom the Lord has had its true effect.

Finally, the Word, the bread that comes, must be eaten or the toiler will grow weak. We are to let this Word of Christ dwell in us, take it into our life. The Word must come into the intellect, the emotion, the will. When we take the Word of God into our whole life and answer its every claim, then in that moment God's purpose will be fulfilled in us.

One of the greatest instruments of God in the world today is the British and Foreign Bible Society. It sends out no preachers, but it accompanies the preacher with his message in the tongue of the people to whom he goes. It cannot issue statistics of conversion, but it pours forth the great stream of living water over all the earth and by such action quenches the thirsts of humanity as with the river of God. Alone, however, it would soon fail. As the Word circulates it becomes the sustenance of human lives, and so over earth's wilderness wastes the green appears that merges at last into the golden glory of the harvests of the Word of God.

NOTES

The Word, a Sword

Charles Haddon Spurgeon (1834–1892) is undoubtedly the most famous minister of the nineteenth century. Converted in 1850, he united with the Baptists and soon began to preach in various places. He became pastor of the Baptist church in Waterbeach, England, in 1851, and three years later he was called to the decaying Park Street Church, London. Within a short time the work began to prosper, a new church was built and dedicated in 1861, and Spurgeon became London's most popular preacher. In 1855, he began to publish his sermons weekly; today they make up the fifty-seven volumes of *The Metropolitan Tabernacle Pulpit*. He founded a pastor's college and several orphanages.

This sermon was taken from *The Metropolitan Tabernacle Pulpit,* volume 34.

Charles Haddon Spurgeon

3

THE WORD, A SWORD

For the word of God is quick, and powerful, and sharper than any two-edged sword, piercing even to the dividing asunder of soul and spirit, and of the joints and marrow, and is a discerner of the thoughts and intents of the heart (Hebrews 4:12).

THOSE WHO ARE fond of a labyrinth of exposition will find a maze perplexing to the last degree if they will read the various commentators and expositors upon this verse. This is the question: By the Word of God, are we here to understand the Incarnate Word, the Divine Logos, who was in the beginning with God; or does the passage relate to this inspired Book and to the Gospel, which is the kernel of it, as it is set forth in the preaching of the truth in the power of the Holy Spirit? You shall find Dr. John Owen, with a very large number of eminent servants of God, defending the first theory that the Son of God is doubtless spoken of here. I confess that they seem to me to defend it with arguments that I should not like to controvert. Much more is to be said on this side of the question than I can here bring before you. On the other side, we find John Calvin, with an equally grand array of divines, all declaring that it must be the Book that is meant, the Gospel, the revelation of God in the Book. Their interpretation of the passage is not to be set aside. I feel convinced that they all give as good reasons for their interpretation as those who come to the other conclusion.

Where such doctors differ, I am not inclined to present any interpretation of my own that can be set in competition with theirs, though I may venture to propound one that comprehends them all and so comes into conflict with none. It is a happy circumstance if we can see a way to agree with all those who did not themselves agree. But

I have been greatly instructed by the mere fact that it should be difficult to know whether in this passage the Holy Spirit is speaking of the Christ of God or the Book of God. This shows us a great truth that we might not otherwise have so clearly noted. How much that can be said of the Lord Jesus may be also said of the inspired volume! How closely are these two allied! How certainly do those who despise the one reject the other! How intimately are the Word made flesh and the Word uttered by inspired men joined together!

It may be most accurate to interpret this passage as relating both to the Word of God incarnate and the Word of God inspired. Weave the two into one thought, for God has joined them together, and you will then see fresh lights and new meanings in the text. The Word of God, namely, this revelation of Himself in Holy Scripture, is all it is here described to be because Jesus, the incarnate Word of God, is in it. He does, as it were, incarnate Himself as the divine truth in this visible and manifest revelation. Thus it becomes living and powerful, dividing and discerning. As the Christ reveals God, so this Book reveals Christ. Therefore it partakes, as the Word of God, in all the attributes of the Incarnate Word. We may say many of the same things of the written Word as of the embodied Word. In fact, they are now so linked together that it would be impossible to divide them.

This I like to think of because there are some nowadays who deny every doctrine of revelation, and yet, forsooth, they praise the Christ. The Teacher is spoken of in the most flattering style, and then His teaching is rejected except so far as it may coincide with the philosophy of the moment. They talk much about Jesus, while that which is the real Jesus—namely, His Gospel and His inspired Word—they cast away. I believe I do but correctly describe them when I say that, like Judas, they betray the Son of Man with a kiss. They even go so far as to cry up the names of the doctrines, though they use them in a different sense that they may deceive. They talk of loyalty to Christ and reverence for the Sermon on the Mount, but they use vain words.

I am charged with sowing suspicion. I do sow it and desire to sow it. Too many Christian people are content to hear anything so long as it is put forth by a clever man in a taking manner. I want them to try the spirits whether they be of God, for many false prophets have gone forth into the world. What God has joined together these modern thinkers willfully put asunder and separate the Revealer from His own revelation. I believe the Savior thinks their homage to be more insulting than their scorn would be. Well may He do so, for they bow before Him and say, "Hail, Master!" while their foot is on the blood of His covenant and their souls abhor the doctrine of His substitutionary sacrifice. They are crucifying the Lord afresh and putting Him to an open shame by denying the Lord that bought them, by daring to deride His purchase of His people as a "mercantile transaction," and I know not what of blasphemy beside.

Christ and His Word must go together. What is true of the Christ is here predicated both of Him and of His Word. Behold, this day the everlasting Gospel has Christ within it. He rides in it as in a chariot. He rides in it as, of old, Jehovah "did ride upon a cherub, and did fly: yes, he did fly upon the wings of the wind." It is only because Jesus is not dead that the Word becomes living and effectual "and sharper than any two-edged sword." If you leave Christ out of it, you have let out its vitality and power. As I have told you that we will not have Christ without the Word, so neither will we have the Word without Christ. If you leave Christ out of Scripture, you have left out the essential truth which it is written to declare. Aye, if you leave out of it Christ as a Substitute, Christ in His death, Christ in His garments dyed in blood, you have left out of it all that is living and powerful.

How often have we reminded you that as concerning the Gospel, even as concerning every man, "the blood is the life thereof." A bloodless gospel is a lifeless gospel! A famous picture has been lately produced that represents our Lord before Pilate. It has deservedly won great attention. A certain excellent newspaper, which brings out for a very cheap price a large number of engravings, has given an engraving of this picture. But, inasmuch as the painting was too large for the paper to give the whole, they have copied a portion of it. It is interesting to note that they have given us Pilate here and Caiaphas there. But since there was no room for Jesus upon the sheet, they have left out that part of the design. When I saw the picture, I thought that it was wonderfully characteristic of a great deal of modern preaching. See Pilate here, Caiaphas there, and the Jews yonder—but the Victim, bound and scourged for human sin, is omitted. Possibly, in the case of the publication, the figure of the Christ will appear in the next number. But even if He would appear in the next sermon of our preachers of the new theology, it will be as a moral example and not as the Substitute for the guilty, the Sin-bearer by whose death we are redeemed.

When we hear a sermon with no Christ in it, we hope that He will come out next Sunday. At the same time, the preaching is, so far, spoiled, and the presentation of the Gospel is entirely ruined so long as the principal fig-ure is left out. Oh, it is a sad thing to have to stand in any house of prayer and listen to the preaching, and then have to cry, "They have taken away my Lord, and I know not where they have laid him"! Rest assured that they have laid Him in a tomb. You may be quite certain of that. They have put Him away as a dead thing, and to them He is as good as dead. True believer, you may com-fort your heart with this recollection, that He will rise again. He cannot be held by the bonds of death in any sense. Though His own church should bury Him and lay the huge lid of the most enormous sarcophagus of her-esy upon Him, the Redeemer will rise again and His truth with Him. He and His Word will live and reign together forever and ever.

Beloved, you will understand I am going to speak about the Word of God as being, like the Lord Jesus, the revelation of God. This inspired volume is that Gospel whereby you have received life, unless you have heard it in vain. It is this Gospel—with Jesus within it, Jesus working by it—that is said to be living and effectual and "sharper than any two-edged sword, piercing even to the dividing asunder of soul and spirit, and of the joints and marrow, and is a discerner of the thoughts and intents of the heart." I shall only talk with you in very simple style. First, *concerning the qualities of the Word of God;* and, secondly, *concerning certain practical lessons that these qualities suggest to us.*

The Qualities of the Word of God

It is "quick and powerful, and sharper than any two-edged sword." The Word of God is said to be *quick*. I am sorry the translators have used that word because it is apt to be mistaken as meaning speedy, and that is not the meaning at all. It means alive or living. "Quick" is the old English word for alive, and so we read of the "quick and dead." The Word of God is alive. This is a living Book. This is a mystery that only living men, quickened by the Spirit of God, will fully comprehend. Take up any other book except the Bible and there may be a measure of power in it, but there is not that indescribable vitality in it that breathes and speaks and pleads and conquers as in the case of this sacred volume.

We have in the book market many excellent selections of choice passages from great authors. In a few instances the persons who have made the extracts have been at the pains to place under their quotations from Scripture the name "David" or "Jesus," but this is worse than needless. There is a style of majesty about God's Word, and with this majesty a vividness never found elsewhere. No other writing has within it a heavenly life whereby it works miracles and even imparts life to its reader. It is a living and incorruptible seed. It moves, it stirs itself, it lives, it communes with living men as a living Word. Solomon said concerning it, "When thou goest, it shall lead thee; when thou sleepest, it shall keep thee; and when thou awakest, it shall talk with thee."

Have you never known what that means? Why, the Book has wrestled with me; the Book has smitten me; the Book has comforted me; the Book has smiled on me; the Book has frowned on me; the Book has clasped my hand; the Book has warmed my heart. The Book weeps with me and sings with me. It whispers to me, and it preaches to me. It maps my way and holds up my goings. It was to me the Young Man's Best Companion, and it is still my Morning and Evening Chaplain. It is a live Book—all over alive. From its first chapter to its last word it is full of a strange, mystic vitality that makes it have preeminence over every other writing for every living child of God.

See, my friends, *our* words, *our* books, our spoken or our printed words by-and-by die out. How many books there are which nobody will ever read now because they are out of date! There are many books that I could read profitably when I was a youth, but they would teach me nothing now. There are also certain religious works that I could read with pleasure during the first ten years of my spiritual life, but I would never think of reading them now anymore than I would think of reading the "a-b ab," and the "b-a ba," of my childhood. Christian experience causes us to outgrow the works that were the class-books of our youth. We may outgrow teachers and pastors, but not apostles and prophets. That human system that was once vigorous and influential may grow old and, at length, lose all vitality. But the Word of God is always fresh and new and full of force. No wrinkle mars its brow; no trembling is in its foot. Here, in the Old and New Testaments, we have at once the oldest and the newest of books. Homer and Hesiod are infants to the more ancient parts of this venerable volume, and yet the Gospel that it contains is as truly *new* as this morning's newspaper. I say again that our words come and go as the trees of the forest multiply their leaves only to cast them off as withered things. So the thoughts and theories of men are but for the season, and then they fade and rot into nothingness. "The grass withereth, and the flower thereof falleth away: but the word of the Lord endureth for ever."

Its vitality is such as it can impart to its readers. Hence, you will often find when you converse with revelation that if you yourself are dead when you begin to read, it does not matter, you will be quickened as you peruse it. You need not bring life *to* the Scripture; you shall draw life *from* the Scripture. Oftentimes a single verse has made us start up, as Lazarus came forth at the call of the Lord Jesus. When our soul has been faint and ready to die, a single word applied to the heart by the Spirit of God has aroused us, for it is a quickening as well as a living Word. I am so glad of this because at times I feel altogether dead. But the Word of God is not dead. And coming to it, we are like the dead man who, when he was put into the grave of the prophet, rose again as soon as he touched his bones. Even these bones of the prophets, these words of theirs spoken and written thousands of years ago, will impart life to those who come into contact with them. The Word of God is thus overflowingly alive.

Hence, I may add it is so alive that you need never be afraid that it will become extinct. They dream—they dream that they have put us among the antiquities, those of us who preach the old Gospel that our fathers loved! They sneer at the doctrines of the apostles and of the reformers. They declare that believers in them are left high and dry, the relics of an age that has long since ebbed away. Yes, so they say! But what they say may not after all be true. For the Gospel is such a living Gospel that if it were cut into a thousand shreds every particle of it would live and grow. If it were buried beneath a thousand avalanches of error, it would shake off the incubus and rise from its grave. If it were cast into the midst of fire, it would walk through the flame, as it has done many times, as though it were in its natural element.

The Reformation was largely due to a copy of the Scriptures left in the seclusion of a monastery. There it was hidden until Luther came under its influence, and his heart furnished soil for the living seed to grow in. Leave but a single New Testament in a popish community and the evangelical faith may at any moment come to the front, even though no preacher of it may ever have come that way. Plants unknown in certain regions have suddenly sprung from the soil. The seeds have been wafted on the winds, carried by birds, or washed ashore by the waves of the sea. So vital are seeds that they live and grow wherever they are borne. Even after lying deep in the soil for centuries, when the upturning spade has brought them to the surface, they have germinated at once. Thus is it with the Word of God: it lives and abides forever. In every soil and under all circumstances it is prepared to prove its own life by the energy with which it grows and produces fruit to the glory of God.

How vain, as well as wicked, are all attempts to kill the Gospel. Those who attempt the crime, in any fashion, will be forever still beginning and never coming near their end. They will be disappointed in all cases whether they would slay it with persecution, smother it with worldliness, crush it with error, starve it with neglect, poison it with misrepresentation, or drown it with infidelity. While God lives, His Word shall live. Let us praise God for that. We have an immortal Gospel incapable of being destroyed, that shall live and shine when the lamp of the sun has consumed its scant supply of oil.

In our text the Word is said to be *powerful* or "active." Perhaps "energetic" is the best rendering, or almost as well, "effectual." Holy Scripture is full of power and energy. Oh, the majesty of the Word of God! They charge us with bibliolatry. It is a crime of their own inventing, of which few are guilty. If there be such things as venial sins, surely an undue reverence of Holy Scripture is one of them. To me the Bible is not God, but it is God's voice, and I do not hear it without awe.

What an honor to have it as one's calling to study, to expound, and to publish this sacred Word! I cannot help feeling that the man who preaches the Word of God is standing not upon a mere platform, but upon a throne. You may study your sermon, my brother, and you may be a great rhetorician and be able to deliver it with wonderful fluency and force. But the only power that is effectual for the highest design of preaching is the power that does not lie in your word, nor in my word, but in the Word of God.

Have you never noticed when persons are converted that they almost always attribute it to some text that was quoted in the sermon? It is God's Word, not our comment on God's Word, that saves souls. The Word of God is powerful for all sacred ends. How powerful it is to convince men of sin! We have seen the self-righteous turned inside out by the revealed truth of God. Nothing else could have brought home to them such unpleasant truth and compelled them to see themselves as in a clear mirror but the searching Word of God.

How powerful it is for conversion! It comes on board a man, and without asking any leave from him, it just puts its hand on the helm and turns him around in the opposite direction from that in which he was going before. The man gladly yields to the irresistible force that influences his understanding and rules his will. The Word of God is that by which sin is slain and grace is born in the heart. It is the light that brings life with it. How active and energetic it is, when the soul is convinced of sin, in bringing it forth into Gospel liberty! We have seen men shut up as in the Devil's own dungeon, and we have tried to get them free. We have shaken the bars of iron, but we could not tear them out so as to set the captives at liberty. But the Word of the Lord is a great breaker of bolts and bars. It not only casts down the strongholds of doubt, but it cuts off the head of Giant Despair. No cell or cellar in Doubting Castle can hold a soul in bondage when the Word of God, which is the master key, is once put to its true use and made to throw back bolts of despondency.

It is living and energetic for encouragement and enlargement. O beloved, what a wonderful power the Gospel has to bring us comfort! It brought us to Christ at the first, and it still leads us to look to Christ until we grow like Him. God's children are not sanctified by legal methods, but by gracious ones. The Word of God, the Gospel of Christ, is exceedingly powerful in promoting sanctification and bringing about that wholehearted consecration that is both our duty and our privilege. May the Lord cause His Word to prove its power in us by its making us fruitful to every good work to do His will!

Through the "washing of water by the Word"—that is, through the washing by the Word—may we be cleansed every day and made to walk in white before the Lord, adorning the doctrine of God our Savior in all things!

The Word of God, then, is quick and powerful in our own personal experience. We shall find it to be so if we use it in laboring to bless our fellowmen. Dear friends, if you seek to do good in this sad world and want a powerful weapon to work with, stick to the Gospel, the living Gospel, the old, old Gospel. There is a power in it sufficient to meet the sin and death of human nature. All the thoughts of men, use them as earnestly as you may, will be like tickling Leviathan with a straw. Nothing can get through the scales of this monster but the Word of God. This is a weapon made of sterner stuff than steel, and it will cut through coats of mail. Nothing can resist it. "Where the word of a king is, there is power." About the Gospel, when spoken with the Holy Spirit sent down from heaven, there is the same omnipotence as there was in the Word of God when in the beginning He spoke to the primeval darkness saying, "Let there be light," and there was light. Oh how we ought to prize and love the revelation of God, not only because it is full of life, but because that life is exceedingly energetic and effectual, and operates so powerfully upon the lives and hearts of men!

Next, the apostle tells us that this Word is *cutting*. "Cutting" would be as correct a translation as that of our own version: it is "more cutting than any two-edged sword." I suppose the apostle means by the description "two-edged" that it is all edge. A sword with two edges has no blunt side. It cuts both this way and that. The revelation of God given us in Holy Scripture is edge all over. It is alive in every part, and in every part keen to cut the conscience and wound the heart. Depend upon it, there is not a superfluous verse in the Bible nor a chapter that is useless. Doctors say of certain drugs that they are *inert*—they have no effect upon the system one way or the other. Now, there is not an inert passage in the Scriptures; every line has its virtues.

Have you never heard of one who heard read, as the

lesson for the Sabbath day, that long chapter of names wherein it is written that each patriarch lived so many hundred years, *"and he died"?* Thus it ends the notice of the long life of Methuselah with "and he died." The repetition of the words, "and he died," woke the thoughtless hearer to a sense of his mortality and led to his coming to the Savior. I would not wonder that away there in the Chronicles among those tough Hebrew names there have been conversions wrought in cases unknown to us as yet.

Anyhow, any bit of Holy Writ is very dangerous to play with. Many a man has been wounded by the Scriptures when he has been idly, or even profanely, reading them. Doubters have meant to break the Word to pieces, and it has broken them. Yes, fools have taken up portions and studied them on purpose to ridicule them, and they have been sobered and vanquished by that which they repeated in sport. There was one who went to hear Mr. Whitefield—a member of the "Hell-fire Club," a desperate fellow. He stood up at the next meeting of his abominable associates and delivered Mr. Whitefield's sermon with wonderful accuracy, imitating his very tone and manner. In the middle of his exhortation he converted himself and came to a sudden pause, sat down brokenhearted, and confessed the power of the Gospel. That club was dissolved. That remarkable convert was Mr. Thorpe of Bristol, whom God so greatly used afterward in the salvation of others. I would rather have you read the Bible to mock at it than not read it at all. I would rather that you came to hear the Word of God out of hatred to it than that you never came at all.

The Word of God is so sharp a thing, so full of cutting power, that you may be bleeding under its wounds before you have seriously suspected the possibility of such a thing. You cannot come near the Gospel without its having a measure of influence over you. God blessing you, it may cut down and kill your sins when you have no idea that such a work is being done. Dear friends, have you not found the Word of God to be very cutting, more cutting than a two-edged sword, so that your heart has bled inwardly, and you have been unable to resist the heavenly stroke? I trust you and I may go on to know more and more of its edge until it has killed us outright, so far as the life of sin is concerned. Oh, to be sacrificed to God, and His Word to be the sacrificial knife! Oh, that His Word were put to the throat of every sinful tendency, every sinful habit, and every sinful thought! There is no sin-killer like the Word of God. Wherever it comes, it comes as a sword and inflicts death upon evil.

Sometimes when we are praying that we may feel the power of the Word, we hardly know what we are praying for. I saw a venerable brother the other day, and he said to me, "I remember speaking with you when you were nineteen or twenty years of age, and I never forgot what you said to me. I had been praying with you in the prayer meeting that God would give us the Holy Spirit to the full. You said to me afterward, 'My dear brother, do you know what you asked God for?' I answered, 'Yes.' But you very solemnly said to me, 'The Holy Spirit is the Spirit of judgment and the Spirit of burning, and few are prepared for the inward conflict that is meant by these two words.'" My good old friend told me that at the time he did not understand what I meant, but thought me a singular youth. "Ah!" said he, "I see it now, but it is only by a painful experience that I have come to the full comprehension of it."

Yes, when Christ comes, He comes not to send peace on the earth, but a sword. And that sword begins at home in our own souls, killing, cutting, hacking, breaking in pieces. Blessed is that man who knows the Word of the Lord by its exceeding sharpness, for it kills nothing but that which ought to be killed. It quickens and gives new life to all that is of God. But the old depraved life that ought to die, it hews in pieces as Samuel destroyed Agag before the Lord. "For the word of God is quick, and powerful, and sharper than any two-edged sword."

But I want you to notice next that it has a further quality: *it is piercing*. While it has an edge like a sword, it has also a point like a rapier, "Piercing even to the dividing asunder of soul and spirit." The difficulty with some men's hearts is to get at them. In fact, there is no spiritually penetrating the heart of any natural man except by this piercing instrument—the Word of God. But the rapier of revelation will go through anything. Even when the "heart is as fat as grease," as the psalmist says, yet this Word will pierce it. Into the very marrow of the man the sacred truth will pass and find him out in a way in which he cannot even find himself out. As it is with our own hearts, so it is with the hearts of other men. Dear friends, the Gospel can find its way anywhere. Men may wrap themselves up in prejudice, but this rapier can find out the joints of their harness. They may resolve not to believe and may feel content in their self-righteousness, but this piercing weapon will find its way. The arrows of the Word of God are sharp in the hearts of the King's enemies, whereby the people fall under Him. Let us not be afraid to trust this weapon whenever we are called up to face the adversaries of the Lord Jesus. We can pin them and pierce them and finish them with this.

And next, *the Word of God is said to be discriminating*. It divides asunder soul and spirit. Nothing else could do that, for the division is difficult. In a great many ways, writers have tried to describe the difference between soul and spirit; but I question whether they have succeeded. No doubt it is a very admirable definition to say, "The soul is the life of the natural man, and the spirit the life of the regenerate or spiritual man." But it is one thing to define and quite another thing to divide.

We will not attempt to solve this metaphysical problem. God's Word comes in, and it shows man the difference between that which is of the soul and that which is of the spirit, that which is of man and that which is of God, that which is of grace and that which is of nature. The Word of God is wonderfully decisive about this. Oh, how much there is of our religion that is—to quote a spiritual poet—"The child of nature finely-dressed, but not the living child." It is of the soul and not of the spirit! The Word of God lays down very straight lines and separates between the natural and the spiritual, the carnal and the divine. You would think sometimes, from the public prayers and preaching of clergymen, that we were all Christian people. But Holy Scripture does not sanction this flattering estimate of our condition. When we are gathered together, the prayers are for us all, and the preaching is for us all, as being all God's people—all born so, or made so by baptism, no question about that! Yet the way the Word of God takes is of quite another sort. It talks about the dead and the living, about the repentant and the impenitent, about the believing and the unbelieving, about the blind and the seeing, about those called of God and those who still lie in the arms of the wicked one. It speaks with keen discrimination and separates the precious from the vile. I believe there is nothing in the world that divides congregations as they ought to be divided like the plain preaching of the Word of God.

This it is that makes our places of worship to be solemn spots, even as Dr. Watts sings—

> Up to her courts with joys unknown
> The holy tribes repair;
> The Son of David holds his throne,
> And sits in judgment there.
>
> He hears our praises and complaints;
> And, while his awful voice
> Divides the sinners from the saints,
> We tremble and rejoice.

The Word of God is discriminating.

Once more, *the Word of God is marvelously revealing to the inner self.* It pierces between the joints and marrow, and marrow is a thing not to be gotten at very readily. The Word of God gets at the very marrow of our manhood; it lays bare the secret thoughts of the soul. It is "a discerner of the thoughts and intents of the heart." Have you not often, in hearing the Word, wondered how the preacher could so unveil that which you had concealed? He says the very things in the pulpit which you had uttered in your bedroom. Yes, that is one of the marks of the Word of God, that it lays bare a man's inmost secrets. Yes, it discovers to him that which he had not even himself perceived. The Christ that is in the

Word sees everything. Read the next verse—"All things are naked and open to the eyes of him with whom we have to do."

The Word not only lets you see what your thoughts are, but it criticizes your thoughts. The Word of God says of this thought, "it is vain," and of that thought, "it is acceptable," of this thought, "it is selfish," and of that thought, "it is Christlike." It is a judge of the thoughts of men. And the Word of God is such a discerner of the thoughts and intents of the heart that when men twist about and wind and wander, yet it tracks them. There is nothing so difficult to get at as a man. You may hunt a badger and run down a fox, but you cannot get at a man—he has so many doublings and hiding places. Yet the Word of God will dig him out and seize on him. When the Spirit of God works with the Gospel, the man may dodge and twist, but the preaching goes to his heart and conscience. He is made to feel it and to yield to its force.

Many times, I do not doubt, dear friends, you have found comfort in the discerning power of the Word. Unkind lips have found great fault with you. You have been trying to do what you could for the Lord, and an enemy has slandered you. Then it has been a delight to remember that the Master discerns your motive. Holy Scripture has made you sure of this by the way in which it understood and commended you. He discerns the true object of your heart and never misinterprets you. This has inspired you with a firm resolve to be the faithful servant of so just a Lord. No slander will survive the judgment seat of Christ. We are not to be tried by the opinions of men, but by the impartial Word of the Lord. Therefore, we rest in peace.

Lessons to Be Gathered from the Qualities of the Word of God

The first is this. Brothers and sisters, *let us greatly reverence the Word of God.* If it be all this, let us read it, study it, prize it, and make it the person of our right hand. And you that are not converted, I do pray you treat the Bible with a holy love and reverence, and read it with the view of finding Christ and His salvation. Augustine used to say that the Scriptures are the swaddling bands of the child Christ Jesus. While you are unrolling the bands, I trust you will meet with Him.

Next, dear friends, let us, *whenever we feel ourselves dead, and especially in prayer, get close to the Word for the Word of God is alive.* I do not find that gracious men always pray alike. Who could? When you have nothing to say to your God, let Him say something to you. The best private devotion is made up half of searching Scripture in which God speaks to us, and the other half of prayer and praise in which we speak to God. When you are dead, turn from your death to that Word, which still lives.

Next, *whenever we feel weak in our duties, let us go to the Word of God, and the Christ in the Word, for power.* This will be the best of power. The power of our natural abilities, the power of our acquired knowledge, the power of our gathered experience, all these may be vanity, but the power that is in the Word will prove effectual. Get up from the cistern of your failing strength to the fountain of omnipotence. For they that drink here—while the youths shall faint and be weary and the young men shall utterly fall—shall run and not be weary, and shall walk and not faint.

Next, *if you need as a minister or a worker anything that will cut your hearers to the heart, go to this Book for it.* I say this because I have known preachers try to use very cutting words of their own. God save us from that! When our hearts grow hot and our words are apt to be sharp as a razor, let us remember that the wrath of man works not the righteousness of God. Let us not attempt to carry on Christ's war with the weapons of Satan. There is nothing so cutting as the Word of God. Keep to that. I believe also that one of the best ways of convincing men of error is not so much to denounce the error as to proclaim the truth more clearly. If a stick is very crooked and you wish to prove that it is so, get a straight one and quietly lay it down by its side. When men look, they will surely see the difference. The Word of God has a very keen edge about it, and all the cutting words you want you had better borrow from there.

And next, *the Word of God is very piercing*. When we cannot get at people by God's truth, we cannot get at them at all. I have heard of preachers who have thought they ought to adapt themselves a little to certain people and leave out portions of the truth that might be disagreeable. Friends, if the Word of God will not pierce, our words will not, you may depend upon *that*. The Word of God is like the sword of Goliath that had been laid up in the sanctuary, of which David said, "There is none like it, give it me." Why did he like it so well? I think he liked it all the better because it had been laid up in the Holy Place by the priests. That is one thing. But I think he liked it best of all because it had stains of blood upon it—the blood of Goliath. I like my own sword because it is covered with blood right up to the hilt. The blood of slaughtered sins and errors and prejudices has made it like the sword of Don Rodrigo, "of a dark and purple tint." The slain of the Lord have been many by the old Gospel. We point to many vanquished by this true Jerusalem blade. They desire me to use a new one. I have not tried it. What have I to do with a weapon that has seen no service? I have proved the Sword of the Lord and of Gideon, and I mean to keep to it. My dear comrades in arms, gird this sword about you and disdain the wooden weapons with which enemies would delude you! Let us use this blade of steel, well tempered in the fire, against the most obstinate, for they cannot stand against it. They may resist it for a time, but they will have to yield. They had better make preparations for surrender. For if the Lord comes out against them with His own Word, they will have to give in and cry to Him for mercy.

Next, if we want to discriminate at any time between the soul and the spirit, and the joints and marrow, *let us go to the Word of God for discrimination*. We need to use the Word of God just now upon several subjects. There is that matter of holiness, upon which one says one thing and another says another. Never mind what they all say; go to the Book, for this is the umpire on all questions. Amidst the controversies of the day about a thousand subjects, keep to this infallible Book and it will guide you unerringly.

And lastly, since this Book is meant to be a discerner or critic of the thoughts and intents of the heart, *let the Book criticize us*. When you have issued a new volume from the press—which you do every day, for every day is a new treatise from the press of life—take it to this great critic, and let the Word of God judge it. If the Word of God approves you, you are approved; if the Word of God disapproves you, you are disapproved. Have friends praised you? They may be your enemies in so doing. Have other observers abused you? They may be wrong or right; let the Book decide. A man of one Book—if that Book is the Bible—is a *man,* for he is a man of God. Cling you to the living Word. Let the Gospel of your fathers, let the Gospel of the martyrs, let the Gospel of the reformers, let the Gospel of the blood-washed multitude before the throne of God, let the Gospel of our Lord Jesus Christ be your Gospel, and none but *that*. It will save you and make you the means of saving others to the praise of God.

NOTES

The Infallibility of Scripture

Charles Haddon Spurgeon (1834–1892) is undoubtedly the most famous minister of the nineteenth century. Converted in 1850, he united with the Baptists and soon began to preach in various places. He became pastor of the Baptist church in Waterbeach, England, in 1851, and three years later he was called to the decaying Park Street Church, London. Within a short time the work began to prosper, a new church was built and dedicated in 1861, and Spurgeon became London's most popular preacher. In 1855, he began to publish his sermons weekly; today they make up the fifty-seven volumes of *The Metropolitan Tabernacle Pulpit*. He founded a pastor's college and several orphanages.

This sermon was taken from *The Metropolitan Tabernacle Pulpit,* volume 34. He preached it on March 11, 1888, the year he left the Baptist Union because of its doctrinal compromise.

4

THE INFALLIBILITY OF SCRIPTURE

The mouth of the LORD hath spoken it (Isaiah 1:20).

WHAT ISAIAH said was, therefore, spoken by Jehovah. It was audibly the utterance of a man; but, really, it was the utterance of the Lord Himself. The lips that delivered the words were those of Isaiah, but yet it was the very truth that "the mouth of the LORD hath spoken it." All Scripture, being inspired of the Spirit, is spoken by the mouth of God. However this sacred Book may be treated nowadays, it was not treated contemptuously nor negligently nor questioningly by the Lord Jesus Christ, our Master and Lord. It is noteworthy how He reverenced the written Word. The Spirit of God rested upon Him personally, without measure. He could speak out of His own mind the revelation of God, and yet He continually quoted the law and the prophets and the Psalms. He always treated the sacred writings with intense reverence, strongly in contrast with the irreverence of "modern thought."

I am sure, friends, we cannot be wrong in imitating the example of our divine Lord in our reverence for that Scripture which cannot be broken. I say, if He—the anointed of the Spirit and able to speak Himself as God's mouth—yet quoted the sacred writings and used the holy Book in His teachings, how much more should we—who have no spirit of prophecy resting upon us and are not able to speak new revelations—come back to the law and to the testimony, and value every single word that "the mouth of the LORD hath spoken"? The like valuation of the Word of the Lord is seen in our Lord's apostles. For they treated the ancient Scriptures as supreme in authority and supported their statements with passages from Holy Writ. The utmost degree of deference and homage is paid to the Old Testament by the writers of the New. We never find an apostle raising a question about the degree of inspiration in this book or that. No disciple of Jesus questions the authority of the books of Moses or of the prophets.

If you want to cavil or suspect, you find no sympathy in the teaching of Jesus or any one of His apostles. The New Testament writers sit reverently down before the Old Testament and receive God's words as such without any question whatsoever. You and I belong to a school that will continue to do the same let others adopt what behavior they please. As for us and for our house, this priceless Book shall remain the standard of our faith and the ground of our hope so long as we live. Others may choose what gods they will and follow what authorities they prefer. But, as for us, the glorious Jehovah is our God, and we believe concerning each doctrine of the entire Bible that "the mouth of the LORD hath spoken it."

This Is Our Warrant for
Teaching Scriptural Truth

We preach because "the mouth of the LORD hath spoken it." It would not be worth our while to speak what Isaiah had spoken if in it there was nothing more than Isaiah's thought. Neither should we care to meditate hour after hour upon the writings of Paul if there was nothing more than Paul in them. We feel no imperative call to expound and to enforce what has been spoken by men. But, since "the mouth of the LORD hath spoken it," it is woe to us if we preach not the Gospel! We come to you with "Thus saith the LORD," and we should have no justifiable motive for preaching our lives away if we have not this message.

The true preacher, the man whom God has commissioned, delivers his message *with awe and trembling* because "the mouth of the LORD hath spoken it." He bears the burden of the Lord and bows under it. Ours is no trifling theme, but one that moves our whole soul. They called George Fox a Quaker because when he spoke he would quake exceedingly through the force of the truth that he so thoroughly apprehended. Perhaps, if you and I had a clearer sight and a closer grip of God's Word and felt more of its majesty, we would quake also. Martin Luther, who never feared the face of man, yet declared that when he stood up to preach he often felt his knees knock together under a sense of his great responsibility. Woe to us if we dare to speak the Word of the Lord with less than our whole heart and soul and strength! Woe to us if we handle the Word as if it were an occasion for display! If it were our own word, we might be studious of the graces of oratory. But if it be God's Word, we cannot afford to think of ourselves. We are bound to speak it, "not with wisdom of words, lest the cross of Christ should be made of none effect." If we reverence the Word, it will not occur to us that we can improve upon it by our own skill in language.

Oh, it were far better to break stones on the road than to be a preacher unless one had God's Holy Spirit to sustain him, for our charge is solemn and our burden is heavy. The heart and soul of the man who speaks for God will know no ease, for he hears in his ears that warning admonition: "If the watchman warn them not they shall perish; but their blood will I require at the watchman's hands." If we were commissioned to repeat the language of a king, we should be bound to do it decorously lest the king suffer damage. But if we rehearse the revelation of God, a profound awe and a godly fear should take hold upon us lest we mar the message of God in the telling of it. No work is so important or honorable as the proclamation of the Gospel of our Lord Jesus. For that very reason it is weighted with a responsibility so solemn that none may venture upon it lightly nor proceed in it without an overwhelming sense of his need of great grace to perform his office aright. We live under intense pressure who preach a Gospel of which we can assuredly say, "The mouth of the LORD hath spoken it." We live rather in eternity than in time. We speak to you as though we saw the great white throne and the divine Judge before whom we must give in our account, not only for what we say, but for how we say it.

Dear friends, because the mouth of the Lord has spoken the truth of God, we therefore endeavor to preach it with *absolute fidelity*. We repeat the Word as a child repeats his lesson. It is not ours to correct the divine revelation, but simply to echo it. I do not take it to be my office to bring you new and original thoughts of my own, but rather to say, "The word which ye hear is not mine, but the Father's which sent me." Believing that "the mouth of the LORD hath spoken it," it is my duty to repeat it to you as correctly as I can after having heard it and felt it in my own soul. It is not mine to amend or adapt the Gospel. What! Shall we attempt to improve upon what God has revealed? The Infinitely Wise—is He to be corrected by creatures of a day? Is the infallible revelation of the infallible Jehovah to be shaped, moderated, and toned down to the fashions and fancies of the hour? God forgive us if we have ever altered His Word unwittingly. Wittingly we have not done so, nor will we.

His children sit at His feet and receive His words, and then they rise up in the power of His Spirit to publish far and near the Word that the Lord has given. "He that hath my word, let him speak my word faithfully" is the Lord's injunction to us. If we could abide with the Father according to our measure after the manner of the Lord Jesus, and then come forth from communion with Him to tell what He has taught us in His Word, we would be accepted of the Lord as preachers. We would also be accepted by His living people far more than if we were to dive into the profound depths of science or rise to the loftiest flights of rhetoric. What is the chaff to the wheat? What are man's discoveries to the teachings of the Lord? "The mouth of the LORD hath spoken it." Therefore, O man of God, add not to His words lest He add to you the plagues that are written in His Book, and take not from them lest He take your name out of the Book of Life!

Again, dear friends, as "the mouth of the LORD hath spoken it," we speak the divine truth *with courage and full assurance*. Modesty is a virtue; but hesitancy when we are speaking for the Lord is a great fault. If an ambassador sent by a great king to represent his majesty at a foreign court should forget his office and only think of himself, he might be so humble as to lower the dignity of his prince, so timid as to betray his country's honor. He is bound to remember not so much what he is in himself, but whom he represents. Therefore, he must speak boldly and with the dignity that is fitting to his office and the court he represents. It was the custom with certain Oriental despots to require ambassadors of foreign powers to lie in the dust before them. Some Europeans, for the sake of trade interests, submitted to the degrading ceremony. But when it was demanded of the representative of England, he scorned thus to lower his country. God forbid that he who speaks for God should dishonor the King of kings by a pliant subservience. We preach not the Gospel by your leave. We do not ask tolerance, nor court applause. We preach Christ crucified, and we speak boldly as we ought to speak because it is God's Word and not our own. We are accused of dogmatism, but we are bound to dogmatize when we repeat that which the mouth of the Lord has spoken. We cannot use "ifs" and "buts," for we are dealing with God's "shalls" and "wills." If He says it is so, it is so; there is an end of it. Controversy ceases when Jehovah speaks.

Those who fling aside our Master's authority may very well reject our testimony. We are content they should do so. But, if we speak that which the mouth of the Lord has spoken, those who hear His Word and refuse it do so at their own peril. The wrong is done, not to the ambassador, but to the King; not to our mouth, but to the mouth of God from whom the truth has proceeded.

We are urged to be charitable. We *are* charitable, but it is with our own money. We have no right to give away what is put into our trust and is not at our disposal. When we have to do with the truth of God, we are stewards. We must deal with our Lord's exchequer, not on the lines of charity to human opinions, but by the rule of fidelity to the God of truth. We are bold to declare with full assurance that which the Lord reveals. That memorable word of the Lord to Jeremiah is needed by the servants of the Lord in these days: "Thou therefore gird up thy loins, and arise, and speak to them all that I command thee: be not dismayed at their faces, lest I confound thee before them. For, behold, I have made thee this day a defenced city, and an iron pillar, and brasen walls against the whole land, against the kings of Judah, against the princes thereof, against the priests thereof, and against the people of the land. And they shall fight against thee; but they shall not prevail against thee; for I am with thee saith the LORD, to deliver thee" (1:17–19). When we speak for the Lord against error, we do not soften our tones; but we speak thunderbolts. When we come across false science, we do not lower our flag. We give place by subjection—no, not for an hour. One word of God is worth more than libraries of human lore. "It is written" is the great gun that silences all the batteries of man's thought. They should speak courageously who speak in the name of Jehovah, the God of Israel.

I will also add under this head that because "the mouth of the LORD hath spoken it," therefore we feel bound to speak His Word *with diligence* as often as ever we can and *with perseverance,* as long as ever we live. Surely, it would be a blessed thing to die in the pulpit, spending one's last breath in acting as the Lord's mouth. Dumb Sabbaths are fierce trials to true preachers. Remember how John Newton, when he was quite unfit to preach and even wandered a bit by reason of his infirmities and age, yet persisted in preaching. When they dissuaded him, he answered with warmth, "What! Shall the old African blasphemer leave off preaching Jesus Christ while there is breath in his body?" So they helped the old man into the pulpit again that he might once more speak of free grace and dying love. If we had common themes to speak about, we might leave the pulpit as a weary pleader quits the forum. But as "the mouth of the LORD hath spoken it," we feel His Word to be a fire in our bones, and we grow more weary with refraining than with testifying. O my friends, the Word of the Lord is so precious that we must in the morning sow this blessed seed, and in the evening we must not withhold our hands. It is a living seed and the seed of life, therefore we must diligently scatter it.

Brethren, if we get a right apprehension concerning Gospel truth—that "the mouth of the LORD hath spoken it"—it will move us to tell it out with *great ardor and zeal*. We shall not drone the Gospel to a slumbering handful. Many of you are not preachers, but you are teachers of the young, or in some other way you try to publish the Word of the Lord—do it, I pray you, with much fervor of Spirit. Enthusiasm should be conspicuous in every servant of the Lord. Let those who hear you know that you are all there, that you are not merely speaking from the lips outwardly. Let them know that from the depths of your soul, your very heart is welling up with a good matter when you speak of things that you have made touching the King. The everlasting Gospel is worth preaching, even if one stood on a burning faggot and addressed the crowd from a pulpit of flames. The truths revealed in Scripture are worth living for and dying for. I count myself thrice happy to bear reproach for the sake of the old faith. It is an honor of which I feel myself to be unworthy. Yet most truly can I use the words of our hymn—

> Shall I, to soothe th' unholy throng,
> Soften thy truths and smooth my tongue?
> To gain earth's gilded toys, or flee
> The cross endured, my God, by thee?
>
> The love of Christ doth me constrain
> To seek the wandering souls of men;
> With cries, entreaties, tears, to save,
> To snatch them from the fiery wave.
>
> My life, my blood I here present,
> If for thy truth they may be spent:
> Fulfil thy sovereign counsel, Lord!
> Thy will be done, thy name adored!

I cannot speak out my whole heart upon this theme that is so dear to me, but I would stir you all up to be instant in season and out of season in telling out the Gospel message. Specially repeat such a word as this: "God so loved the world, that he gave his only begotten Son, that whosoever believeth in him should not perish, but have everlasting life." And this: "Him that cometh to me I will in no wise cast out." Tell it out boldly, tell it out in every place, tell it out to every creature, "For the mouth of the LORD hath spoken it." How can you keep back the heavenly news? "The mouth of the LORD hath spoken it"—shall not your mouth rejoice to repeat it? Whisper it in the ear of the sick, shout it in the corner of the streets, write it on your tablets, send it forth from the press, but everywhere let this be your great motive and warrant—you preach the Gospel because "the mouth of the LORD hath spoken it." Let nothing be silent that has a voice when the Lord has given the Word by His own dear Son.

> Waft, waft, ye winds his story,
>   And you, ye waters, roll,
> Till like a sea of glory
>   It spreads from pole to pole.

This Is the Claim of God's Word Upon Your Attention

Every word that God has given us in this Book claims our attention, because of the *infinite majesty of Him that spoke it*. I see before me a parliament of kings and princes, sages and senators. I hear one after another of the gifted Chrysostoms pour forth eloquence like the "golden-mouthed." They speak, and they speak well. Suddenly, there is a solemn hush. What a stillness! Who is now to speak? They are silent because God the Lord is about to lift up His voice. Is it not right that they should be so? Does He not say, "Keep silence before me, O islands"? What voice is like His voice? "The voice of the Lord is powerful; the voice of the Lord is full of majesty. The voice of the Lord breaketh the cedars; yes, the Lord breaketh the cedars of Lebanon. The voice of the Lord shaketh the wilderness; the Lord shaketh the wilderness of Kadesh." See that you do not refuse Him that speaks.

O my hearer, let it not be said of you that you went through this life, God speaking to you in His Book, and you refusing to hear! It matters very little whether you listen to me or not. But it matters a very great deal whether you listen to God or not. It is He that made you, and in His hands is your breath. If He speaks, I implore you, open your ear and be not rebellious. There is an infinite majesty about every line of Scripture, but especially about that part of Scripture in which the Lord reveals Himself and His glorious plan of saving grace in the person of His dear Son Jesus Christ. The cross of Christ has a great claim upon you. Hear what Jesus preaches from the tree. He says, "Incline your ear, and come to me: hear, and your soul shall live."

God's claim to be heard lies, also, in *the condescension that has led Him to speak to us*. It was something for God to have made the world and bid us look at the work of His hands. Creation is a picture book for children. But for God to speak in the language of mortal men is still more marvelous, if you come to think of it. I wonder that God spoke by the prophets. But I admire still more that He should have written down His word in black and white, in unmistakable language that can be translated into all tongues so that we may all see and read for ourselves what God the Lord has spoken to us and what, indeed, He continues to speak. For what He has spoken He still speaks to us as freshly as if He spoke it for the first time. O glorious Jehovah, do You speak to mortal man? Can there be any that neglect to hear You? If You are so full of lovingkindness and tenderness that You will stoop out of heaven to converse with Your sinful creatures, none but those who are more brutal than the ox and the donkey will turn a deaf ear to You!

God's Word has a claim, then, upon your attention because of its majesty and its condescension. But yet, further, it should win your ear because of *its intrinsic importance*. "The mouth of the LORD hath spoken it"—then it is no trifle. God never speaks vanity. No line of His writing treats of the frivolous themes of a day. That which may be forgotten in an hour is for mortal man and not for the eternal God. When the Lord speaks, His speech is Godlike. Its themes are worthy of one whose dwelling is infinity and eternity. God does not play with you, human. Will you trifle with Him? Will you treat Him as if He were altogether such a one as yourself? God is in earnest when He speaks to you. Will you not in earnest listen? He speaks to you of great things that have to do with your soul and its destiny. "It is not a vain thing for you; because it is your life." Your eternal existence, your happiness or your misery, hang on your treatment of that which the mouth of the Lord has spoken. Concerning eternal realities He speaks to you. I pray, be not so unwise as to turn away your ear. Act not as if the Lord and His truth were nothing to you. Treat not the Word of the Lord as a secondary thing that might wait your leisure and receive attention when no other work was before you. Put all else aside, but hearken to your God.

Depend upon it, if "the mouth of the LORD hath spoken it," there is an urgent, pressing necessity. God breaks not silence to say that which might as well have remained unsaid. His voice indicates great urgency. Today, if you will hear His voice, hear it—for He demands immediate attention. God does not speak without abundant reason. O my hearer, if He speaks to you by His Word, I beseech you, believe that there must be overwhelming cause for it! I know what Satan says. He tells you that you can do very well without listening to God's Word. I know what your carnal heart whispers. It says, "Listen to the voice of business and of pleasure, but listen not to God." But, oh! if the Holy Spirit shall teach your reason to be reasonable and put your mind in mind of true wisdom, you will acknowledge that the first thing you have to do is to heed your Maker. You can hear the voices of others another time. But your ear must hear God first, since He is first and that which He speaks must be of first importance. Without delay do you make haste to keep His commandments. Without reserve answer to His call and say, "Speak, Lord; for thy servant heareth."

When I stand in this pulpit to preach the Gospel, I never feel that I may calmly invite you to attend to a subject that is one among many, and may very properly be let alone for a time should your minds be already occupied. No, you may be dead before I again speak with you, and so I beg for immediate attention. I do not fear that I may be taking you off from other important business by entreating you to attend to that which the mouth of the Lord has spoken. For no business has any importance in it compared with this. This is the master theme of all. It is your soul, your own soul, your ever-existing soul that is concerned, and it is your God that is speaking to you. Do hear Him, I beseech you. I am not asking a favor of you when I request you to hear the Word of the Lord. It is a debt to your Maker that you are bound to pay. Yes, it is, moreover, kindness to your own self. Even from a selfish point of view, I urge you to hear what the mouth of the Lord has spoken, for in His Word lies salvation. Hearken diligently to what your Maker, your Savior, your best friend, has to say to you. "Harden not your hearts, as in the provocation," but "incline your ear, and come to me: hear, and your soul shall live." "Faith cometh by hearing, and hearing by the Word of God."

Thus I have handled my text in two ways: it is warrant and motive for the preacher; it is a demand upon the attention of the hearer.

This Gives to God's Word a Very Special Character

When we open this sacred Book and say of that which is here recorded, "the mouth of the LORD hath spoken it," then it gives to the teaching a special character.

In the Word of God the teaching has *unique dignity*. This Book is inspired as no other book is inspired, and it is time that all Christians avowed this conviction. I do not know whether you have seen Mr. Smiles' life of our late friend, George Moore. But in it we read that, at a certain dinner party, a learned man remarked that it would not be easy to find a person of intelligence who believed in the inspiration of the Bible. In an instant George Moore's voice was heard across the table saying boldly, "I do, for one." Nothing more was said. My dear friend had a strong way of speaking, as I well remember, for we have upon occasions vied with each other in shouting when we were together at his Cumberland home. I think I can hear his emphatic way of putting it:

"I do, for one." Let us not be backward to take the old-fashioned and unpopular side, and say outright, "I do, for one." Where are we if our Bibles are gone? Where are we if we are taught to distrust them? If we are left in doubt as to which part is inspired and which is not, we are as badly off as if we had no Bible at all.

I hold no theory of inspiration; I accept the inspiration of the Scriptures as a fact. Those who thus view the Scriptures need not be ashamed of their company, for some of the best and most learned of men have been of the same mind. Locke, the great philosopher, spent the last fourteen years of his life in the study of the Bible. When asked what was the shortest way for a young gentleman to understand the Christian religion, he bade him read the Bible, remarking: "Therein are contained the words of eternal life. It has God for its author, salvation for its end, and truth, without any admixture of error, for its matter." There are those on the side of God's Word whom you need not be ashamed of in the matter of intelligence and learning. If it were not so, it should not discourage you when you remember that the Lord has hid these things from the wise and prudent, and has revealed them to babes. We believe with the apostle that "the foolishness of God is wiser than men." It is better to believe what comes out of God's mouth and be called a fool than to believe what comes out of the mouth of philosophers and be, therefore, esteemed a wise man.

There is also about that which the mouth of the Lord has spoken an *absolute certainty*. What man has said is unsubstantial, even when true. It is like grasping fog, there is nothing of it. But with God's Word you have something to grip at, something to have and to hold. This is substance and reality. But of human opinions we may say, "Vanity of vanities, all is vanity." Though heaven and earth should pass away, yet not one jot or tittle of what God has spoken shall fail. We know that, and feel at rest. God cannot be mistaken. God cannot lie. These are postulates that no one can dispute. If "the mouth of the Lord hath spoken it," this is the judge that ends the strife where wit and reason fall; henceforth, we question no more.

Again: if "the mouth of the LORD hath spoken it," we have in this utterance the special character of *immutable fixedness*. Once spoken by God, not only is it so now, but it always must be so. The Lord of Hosts has spoken, and who shall disannul it? The rock of God's Word does not shift like the quicksand of modern scientific theology. One said to his minister, "My dear sir, surely you ought to adjust your beliefs to the progress of science." "Yes," said he, "but I have not had time to do it today for I have not yet read the morning papers." One would have need to read the morning papers and take in every new edition to know where about scientific theology now stands, for it is always chopping and changing. The only thing that is certain about the false science of this age is that it will be soon disproved. Theories vaunted today will be scouted tomorrow. The great scientists live by killing those who went before them. They know nothing for certain, except that their predecessors were wrong. Even in one short life we have seen system after system—the mushrooms, or rather the toadstools, of thought—rise and perish. We cannot adapt our religious belief to that which is more changeful than the moon. Try it who will. As for me, if "the mouth of the LORD hath spoken it," it is truth to me in this year of grace 1888. And if I stand among you a gray-headed old man somewhere in 1908, you will find me making no advance upon the divine ultimatum. If "the mouth of the LORD hath spoken it," we behold in His revelation a Gospel which is without variableness, revealing "Jesus Christ, the same yesterday, today, and for ever." Brothers and sisters, we hope to be together forever before the eternal throne where bow the blazing Seraphim. Even then we shall not be ashamed to avow that same truth that this day we feed upon from the hand of our God.

> For he's the Lord, supremely good,
> His mercy is for ever sure;
> His truth, which always firmly stood,
> To endless ages shall endure.

Here let me add that there is something unique about

God's Word because of the almighty power that attends it. "Where the word of a king is, there is power." Where the word of a God is, there is omnipotence. If we dealt more largely in God's own Word as "the mouth of the LORD hath spoken it," we should see far greater results from our preaching. It is God's Word, not our comment on God's Word, that saves souls. Souls are slain by the sword, not by the scabbard nor by the tassels that adorn the hilt of it. If God's Word be brought forward in its native simplicity, no one can stand against it. The adversaries of God must fail before the Word as chaff perishes in the fire. Oh, for wisdom to keep closer and closer to that which the mouth of the Lord has spoken!

I will say no more on this point, although the theme is a very large and tempting one—especially if I were to dwell upon the depth, the height, the adaptation, the insight, and the self-proving power of that which "the mouth of the LORD hath spoken."

This Makes God's Word a Ground of Great Alarm to Many

Shall I read you the whole verse? "But if ye refuse and rebel, ye shall be devoured with the sword: for the mouth of the LORD hath spoken it." Every threat that God has spoken, because He has spoken it, has a tremendous dread about it. Whether God threatens a man or a nation or the whole class of the ungodly, if they are wise they will feel a trembling take hold upon them because "the mouth of the LORD hath spoken it." *God has never yet spoken a threat that has fallen to the ground.* When He told Pharaoh what He would do, He did it. The plagues came thick and heavy upon him. When the Lord at any time sent His prophets to denounce judgments on the nations, He carried out those judgments. Ask travelers concerning Babylon, Nineveh, Edom, Moab, and Bashan, and they will tell you of the heaps of ruins that prove how the Lord carried out His warnings to the letter.

One of the most awful things recorded in history is the siege of Jerusalem. You have read it, I do not doubt, in Josephus or elsewhere. It makes one's blood run cold to think of it. Yet it was all foretold by the prophets, and their prophecies were fulfilled to the bitter end. You talk about God as being "love." If you mean by this that He is not severe in the punishment of sin, I ask you what you make of the destruction of Jerusalem. Remember that the Jews were His chosen nation and that the city of Jerusalem was the place where His temple had been glorified with His presence.

Friends, if you roam from Edom to Zion, and from Zion to Sidon, and from Sidon to Moab, you will find amid ruined cities the tokens that God's words of judgment are sure. Depend on it, then, that when Jesus says, "These shall go away into everlasting punishment," it will be so. When He says "If ye believe not that I am he, ye shall die in your sins," it will be so. The Lord never plays at frightening us. His Word is not an exaggeration to scare people with imaginary bugbears. There is emphatic truth in what the Lord says. He has always carried out His threats to the letter and to the moment. Depend upon it, He will continue to do so, "For the mouth of the LORD hath spoken it."

It is of no avail to sit down and draw inferences from the nature of God and to argue "God is love, and therefore he will not execute the sentence upon the impenitent." He knows what He will do better than you can infer. He has not left us to inferences, for He has spoken pointedly and plainly. He says, "He that believeth not shall be damned," and it will be so, "For the mouth of the LORD hath spoken it." Infer what you like from His nature, but if you draw an inference contrary to what He has spoken, you have inferred a lie and will find it so.

"Alas," says one, "I shudder at the severity of the divine sentence." Do you? It is well! I can heartily sympathize with you. What must he be that does not tremble when he sees the great Jehovah taking vengeance upon iniquity! The terrors of the Lord might well turn steel to wax. Let us remember that the gauge of truth is not our pleasure nor our terror. It is not my shuddering that can disprove what the mouth of the Lord has spoken. It may even be a proof of its truth. Did not all the prophets tremble at manifestations of God? Remember how one of them cried: "When I heard, my belly trembled; my lips quivered at the voice; rottenness entered into my bones." One of the last of the anointed seers fell at the Lord's feet as dead. Yet all the shrinking of their nature was not used by them as an argument for doubt.

O my unconverted and unbelieving hearers, do remember that if you refuse Christ and rush upon the keen edge of Jehovah's sword, your unbelief of eternal judgment will not alter it nor save you from it. I know why you do not believe in the terrible threatenings. It is because you want to be easy in your sins. A certain skeptical writer, when in prison, was visited by a Christian man who wished him well. But he refused to hear a word about religion. Seeing a Bible in the hand of his visitor, he made this remark, "You do not expect me to believe in that book, do you? Why, if that book is true, I am lost forever." Just so. Therein lies the reason for half the infidelity in the world and all the infidelity in our congregations. How can you believe that which condemns you? Ah! my friends, if you would believe it to be true and act accordingly, you would also find in that which the mouth of the Lord has spoken a way of escape from the wrath to come, for the Book is far more full of hope than of dread. This inspired volume flows with the milk of mercy and the honey of grace. It is not a Doomsday Book of wrath, but a testament of grace. Yet, if you do not believe its loving warnings, nor regard its just sentences, they are true all the same. If you dare its thunders, if you trample on its promises, and even if you burn it in your rage, the holy Book still stands unaltered and unalterable, for "the mouth of the LORD hath spoken it." Therefore, I pray you, treat the sacred Scriptures with respect. Remember that "These are written, that ye might believe that Jesus is the Christ, the Son of God; and that believing ye might have life through his name."

This Makes the Word of the Lord the Reason and Rest of Our Faith

"The mouth of the LORD hath spoken it," is the foundation of our confidence. There is forgiveness, for God has said it. Look, friend, you are saying, "I cannot believe that my sins can be washed away. I feel so unworthy." Yes, but "the mouth of the Lord hath spoken it." Believe over the head of your unworthiness. "Ah," says one, "I feel so weak I can neither think, nor pray, nor anything else, as I should." Is it not written, "When we were yet without strength, in due time Christ died for the ungodly"? "The mouth of the Lord hath spoken it"; therefore, over the head of your inability still believe it, for it must be so.

I think I hear some child of God saying, "God has said, 'I will never leave thee, nor forsake thee.' But I am in great trouble. All the circumstances of my life seem to contradict the promise." Yet, "the mouth of the Lord hath spoken it," and the promise must stand. "Trust in the Lord, and do good; so shalt thou dwell in the land, and verily thou shalt be fed." Believe God in the teeth of circumstances. If you cannot see a way of escape or a means of help, yet still believe in the unseen God and in the truth of His presence; "For the mouth of the Lord hath spoken it." I think I have come to this pass with myself, at any rate for the time present, that when circumstances deny the promise, I believe it nonetheless. When friends forsake me and foes belie me—when my own spirit goes down below zero and I am depressed almost to despair— I am resolved to hang to the bare Word of the Lord and prove it to be in itself an all-sufficient stay and support. I will believe God against all the devils in hell—God against Ahithophel, Judas, Demas, and all the rest of the turncoats—yes, and God against my own evil heart. His purpose shall stand, "for the mouth of the Lord hath spoken it." Away, you that contradict it. Ours is a well-grounded confidence, "for the mouth of the Lord hath spoken it."

By-and-by we shall come to die. The death-sweat shall gather on our brow, and perhaps our tongue will scarcely serve us. Oh that then, like the grand old German emperor, we may say, "Mine eyes have seen thy salvation," and, "He hath helped me with his name." When we pass through the rivers, He will be with us. The floods shall not overflow us, "for the mouth of the LORD hath spoken it." When we walk through the valley of the shadow of death, we shall fear no evil, for He will be with us. His rod and His staff shall comfort us. "The mouth of the LORD hath spoken it." Ah! what will it be to break loose from these bonds and rise into the glory? We shall soon see the King in His beauty and be ourselves glorified in His glory, "for the mouth of the LORD hath spoken it." "He that believeth hath everlasting life," therefore a glad eternity is ours.

Friends, we have not followed cunningly devised fables. We are not "wanton boys that swim on bladders," which will soon burst under us. But we are resting on firm ground. We abide where heaven and earth are resting, where the whole universe depends, where even eternal things have their foundation—we rest on God Himself. If God shall fail us, we gloriously fail with the whole universe. But there is no fear. Therefore let us trust and not be afraid. His promise must stand, "for the mouth of the LORD hath spoken it." O Lord, it is enough. Glory be to Your name through Christ Jesus! Amen.

NOTES

The Bible Is Right

Thomas DeWitt Talmage (1832–1902) was studying law when he sensed a call to ministry; and after completing his studies at New Brunswick Seminary in 1856, he was ordained in the Dutch Reformed Church. He pastored both Reformed and Presbyterian churches and also served as chaplain in the Union Army. In 1870, his congregation at Central Presbyterian Church, Brooklyn, New York, erected a four-thousand seat auditorium that became known as "The Brooklyn Tabernacle." He ministered there for twenty-five years. From 1895 to 1899, he served as associate pastor of the First Presbyterian Church, Washington, D.C., retiring in 1899. His sermons were published in over three thousand newspapers in the United States and overseas. He was widely recognized as a gifted pulpit orator who was unashamed of the Gospel.

This sermon was taken from volume 7 of "The Great Pulpit Masters" series published in 1951 by Fleming H. Revell.

Thomas DeWitt Talmage

5

THE BIBLE IS RIGHT

The statutes of the LORD are right (Psalm 19:8).

OLD BOOKS go out of date. When they were written, they discussed questions that were being discussed. They struck at wrongs that had long ago ceased, or advocated institutions that excite not our interest. Were they books of history, the facts had been gathered from the imperfect mass, better classified and more lucidly presented. Were they books of poetry, they were interlocked with wild mythologies that have gone up from the face of the earth like mists at sunrise. Were they books of morals, civilization will not sit at the feet of barbarism, neither do we want Sappho, Pythagoras, and Tully to teach us morals. What do the masses of people care now for the pathos of Simonides or the sarcasm of Menander or the gracefulness of Philemon or the wit of Aristophanes? Even the old books we have left, with a few exceptions, have but very little effect upon our times. Books are human. They have a time to be born, are fondled, grow in strength, have a middle-life of usefulness. Then comes old age, they totter and die. Many of the national libraries are merely the cemeteries of dead books. Some of them lived flagitious lives and died deaths of ignominy. Some were virtuous and accomplished a glorious mission. Some went into the ashes through inquisitorial fires. Some found their funeral pile in sacked and plundered cities. Some were neglected and died as foundlings at the door of science. Sooner or later there comes into your possession an old book, its author forgotten and its usefulness done. With leathern lips it seems to say: "I wish I were dead." Monuments have been raised over poets and philanthropists. Would that some tall shaft might be erected in honor of the world's buried books.

The world's authors would make pilgrimage thereto, and poetry and literature and science and religion would consecrate it with their tears.

Not so with one old book. It started in the world's infancy. It grew under theocracy and monarchy. It withstood storms of fire. It grew under the prophet's mantle and under the fisherman's coat of the apostles—in Rome and Ephesus and Jerusalem and Patmos. Tyranny issued edicts against it, and infidelity put out the tongue. Mohammedanism from its mosques hurled its anathemas, but the old Bible lived. It crossed the British Channel and was greeted by Wyclif and James I. It crossed the Atlantic and struck Plymouth Rock, until like that of Horeb it gushed with blessedness. Churches and asylums have gathered all along its way, ringing their bells and stretching out their hands of blessing. And every Sabbath there are ten thousand heralds of the Cross with their hands on this open, grand, free, old English Bible. But it will not have accomplished its mission until it has climbed the icy mountains of Greenland, gone over the granite cliffs of China, thrown its glow amid the Australian mines, or scattered its gems among the diamond districts of Brazil. All thrones shall be gathered into one throne, and all crowns by the fires of revolution shall be melted into one crown, and this Book shall at the very gate of heaven have waved in the ransomed empires—not until then will this glorious Bible have accomplished its mission.

In carrying out, then, the idea of my text—"The statutes of the Lord are right"—I shall show you that the Bible is right in authentication, style, doctrine, and effects.

The Bible Is Right in Its Authentication

Can you doubt the authenticity of the Scriptures? There is not so much evidence that Walter Scott wrote "The Lady of the Lake," not so much evidence that Shakespeare wrote "Hamlet," not so much evidence that John Milton wrote "Paradise Lost," as there is evidence that the Lord God Almighty—by the hands of the prophets, evangelists, and apostles—wrote this Book. Suppose a book now to be written came in conflict with a great many things and was written by bad men or impostors, how long would such a book stand? It would be scouted by everybody. And I say, if the Bible had been an imposition—if it had not been written by the men who said they wrote it—if it had been a mere collection of falsehoods—do you not suppose that it would have been immediately rejected by the people? If Job, Isaiah, Jeremiah, Paul, Peter, and John were impostors, they would have been scouted by generations and nations. If that Book has come down through fires of centuries without a scar, it is because there is nothing in it destructible.

How near have they come to destroying the Bible? When they began their opposition, there were two or three thousand copies of it. Now there are two hundred million, so far as I can calculate. These Bible truths, notwithstanding all the opposition, have gone into all languages—into the philosophic Greek, the flowing Italian, the graceful German, the passionate French, the picturesque Indian, and the exhaustless Anglo-Saxon. Under the painter's pencil, the birth and the Crucifixion and the Resurrection glow on the walls of palaces. Under the engraver's knife they speak from the mantel of the mountain cabin, while stones, touched by the sculptor's chisel, start up into preaching apostles and ascending martyrs. Now, do you not suppose, if that Book had been an imposition and a falsehood, it would have gone down under these ceaseless fires of opposition?

Further, suppose that there was a great pestilence going over the earth, and hundreds of thousands of men were dying of that pestilence. Suppose someone should find a medicine that cured ten thousand people, would not everybody acknowledge that that must be a good medicine? Why, someone would say: "Do you deny it? There have been ten thousand people cured by it." I simply state the fact that there have been hundreds of thousands of Christian men and women who say they have felt the truthfulness of that Book and its power in their souls. It has cured them of the worst leprosy that ever came down on our earth, namely, the leprosy of sin. If I can point you to multitudes who say they have felt the power of that cure, are you not reasonable enough to acknowledge the fact that there must be some power in the medicine? Will you take the evidence of millions of patients who have been cured? Or will you take the evidence of the skeptic who stands aloof and confesses that he never took the medicine?

The Bible intimates that there was a city called Petra, built out of solid rock. Infidelity scoffed at it. "Where is your city of Petra?" Buckhardt and Laborde went forth in their explorations, and they came upon that very city. The mountains stand around like giants guarding the tomb where the city is buried. They find a street in that city six miles long where once flashed imperial pomp and which echoed with the laughter of lighthearted mirth on its way to the theater. On temples, fashioned out of colored stones—some of which have blushed into the crimson of the rose and some of which have darkened into the blue of the sky and some of which have paled into the whiteness of the lily—aye, on column and pediment and entablature and statuary, God writes the truth of that Bible.

The Bible says that Sodom and Gomorrah were destroyed by fire and brimstone. "Absurd." Infidels, year after year, have said: "It is positively absurd that they could have been destroyed by brimstone. There is nothing in the elements to cause such a shower of death as that." Lieutenant Lynch—I think he was the first man who went out on the discovery, but he has been followed by many others—Lieutenant Lynch went out in exploration and came to the Dead Sea, which, by a convulsion of nature, has overflowed the place where the cities once stood. He sank his fathoming line and brought up from the bottom of the Dead Sea great masses of sulfur, remnants of that very tempest that swept Sodom and Gomorrah to ruin. Who was right—the Bible that announced the destruction of those cities, or the skeptics who for ages scoffed at it?

The Bible says there was a city called Nineveh, that

it was three days' journey around it, and that it should be destroyed by fire and water. "Absurd," cried out hundreds of voices for many years. "No such a city was ever built that it would take you three days' journey to go around. Besides, it could not be destroyed by fire and water. They are antagonistic elements." But Layard, Botta, Bonomi, and Keith go out, and by their explorations they find that city of Nineveh. They tell us that by their own experiment it is three days' journey around (according to the old estimate of a day's journey). They also tell us that it was literally destroyed by fire and by water—two antagonistic elements. A part of the city having been inundated by the river Tigris (the brick material in those times being dried clay instead of burned); while in other parts they find the remains of the fire in heaps of charcoal that have been excavated and in the calcined slabs of gypsum. Who was right, the Bible or infidelity?

Moses intimated that they had vineyards in Egypt. "Absurd," cried hundreds of voices. "You can't raise grapes in Egypt. Or, if you can, it is a very great exception that you can raise them." But the traveler goes down, and in the underground vaults of Eilithya he finds painted on the wall all the process of tending the vines and treading out the grapes. It is all there, familiarly sketched by people who evidently knew all about it and saw it all about them every day. In those underground vaults there are vases still encrusted with the settlings of the wine. You see the vine *did* grow in Egypt, whether it grows there *now* or not.

Thus you see, while God wrote the Bible, at the same time He wrote this commentary: "The statutes of the LORD are right." He wrote it on leaves of rock and shell, bound in clasps of metal, lying on mountain tables, and in the jeweled vase of the sea. In authenticity and in genuiness "the statutes of the LORD are right."

The Bible Is Right in Its Style

I know there are a great many people who think it is merely a collection of genealogical tables and dry facts.

That is because they do not know how to read the Book. You take up the most interesting novel that was ever written. If you commence at the four hundredth page today, and tomorrow at the three hundredth, and the next day at the first page, how much sense or interest would you gather from it? Yet that is the very process to which the Bible is subjected every day. An angel from heaven, reading the Bible in that way, could not understand it. The Bible has a door by which to enter and a door by which to go out. Genesis is the door to go in and Revelation the door to go out. These Epistles of Paul the apostle are merely letters written, folded up, and sent by postmen to the different churches. Do you read other letters the way you read Paul's letters? Suppose you get a business letter, and you know that in it there are important financial propositions. Do you read the last page first, and then one line of the third page, and another of the second, and another of the first? No. You begin with "Dear Sir," and end with "Yours truly."

Now, here is a letter written from the throne of God to our lost world. It is full of magnificent hopes and propositions. We dip in here and there, and we know nothing about it. Besides that, people read the Bible when they cannot do anything else. It is a dark day, and they do not feel well. They do not go about their normal business, so after lounging about a while they pick up the Bible—their mind refuses to enjoy the truth. Or they come home weary from the store or shop, and they feel, if they do not say, it is a dull book. While the Bible is to be read on stormy days and while your head aches, it is also to be read in the sunshine and when your nerves, like harpstrings, thrum the song of health. While your vision is clear walk in this paradise of truth. While your mental appetite is good pluck these clusters of grace.

I am fascinated with the conciseness of this book. Every word is packed full of truth. Every sentence is doublebarreled. Every paragraph is like an old banyan tree, with a hundred roots and a hundred branches. It is a great arch; pull out one stone and it all comes down. There has never been a pearl diver who could gather up one half of the treasures in any verse. John Halsebach of Vienna for twenty-one years every Sabbath, expounded to his congregation the first chapter of the book of Isaiah and yet did not get through with it. Nine-tenths of all the good literature of this age is merely the Bible diluted.

I am also amazed at the variety of this Book. Mind you, not contradiction or collision, but variety. Just as in the song you have the bass and alto and soprano and tenor—they are not in collision with each other, but come in to make up the harmony—so it is in this Book. There are different parts of this great song of redemption. The prophet comes and takes one part, the patriarch another part, and the evangelist another part, the apostles another part, and yet they all come into the grand harmony—the song of "Moses and the Lamb." If God had inspired men of the same temperament to write this Book, it might have been monotonous. But David, Isaiah, Peter, Job, Ezekiel, Paul, and John were men of different temperaments. So, when God inspired them to write, they wrote in their own style.

God prepared the Book for all classes of people. For instance, little children would read the Bible and God knew that. Therefore, He allowed Matthew and Luke to write sweet stories about Christ—with the doctors of the law, and Christ at the well, and Christ at the cross—so that any little child can understand them. Then God knew that the aged people would want to read the Book, so He allowed Solomon to compact a world of wisdom in that book of Proverbs. God knew that the historian would want to read it, so He allowed Moses to give the plain statements of the Pentateuch. God knew that the poet would want to read it, so He allowed Job to picture the heavens as a curtain, and Isaiah the mountains as weighed in a balance and the waters as held in the hollow of the omnipotent hand.

And God touched David, until in the latter part of the Psalms, he gathered a great choir standing in galleries above each other. There were beasts and men in the first gallery. Above them were hills and mountains. Above them were fire and hail and tempest. Above them were sun and moon and stars of light. Then, on the highest gallery, arrayed the hosts of angels. Then, standing before this great choir, reaching from the depths of earth to the heights of heaven, he lifts his hands like the leader of a great orchestra crying: "Praise ye the LORD. Let everything that hath breath praise the LORD." And all earthly creatures in their song, mountains with their waving cedars, tempests in their thunder and rattling hail, stars on all their trembling harps of light, and angels on their thrones respond in magnificent acclaim: "Praise ye the LORD. Let everything that hath breath praise the LORD."

God knew that the pensive and complaining world would want to read it, so He inspired Jeremiah to write: "Oh that my head were waters, and mine eyes a fountain of tears." God knew that the lovers of the wild, romantic, and the strange would want to read it, so He let Ezekiel write of mysterious rolls, winged creatures, and flying wheels of fire. God prepared it for all zones—for the Arctic and the tropics, as well as for the temperate zone. Cold-blooded Greenlanders would find much to interest them, and the tanned inhabitant at the equator would find his passionate nature boil with the vehemence of heavenly truth. The Arabian would read it on his dromedary, the Laplander seated on the swift sled, the herdsman of Holland guarding the cattle in the grass, and the Swiss girl reclining amid Alpine crags. Oh, when I see that the Bible is suited in style—exactly suited to all ages, to all conditions, to all lands—I cannot help repeating the conclusion of my text: "The statutes of the LORD are right."

The Bible Is Right in Its Doctrine

Man a sinner, Christ a Savior—the two doctrines. Man must come down—his pride, his self-righteousness, his worldliness. Christ, the Anointed, must go up. If it had not been for the setting forth of the atonement, Moses would never have described the creation, prophets would not have predicted, apostles would not have preached.

It seems to me as if Jesus, in the Bible, was standing on a platform in a great amphitheater. The prophets were behind Him throwing light forward on His sacred person, and the apostles and evangelists stood before Him like footlights throwing up their light into His blessed countenance. Then it seems as if all the earth and heaven were the applauding auditory. The Bible speaks of Pisgah and Carmel, and Sinai, but makes all mountains bow down to Calvary. The flocks led over the Judean hills were emblems of "the lamb of God that taketh away the sin of the world," and the lion leaping out of its lair was an emblem of "the lion of Judah's tribe."

I will, in my next breath, recite to you the most wonderful sentence ever written: "This is a faithful saying, and worthy of all acceptation, that Christ Jesus came into the world to save sinners." No wonder that when Jesus was born in Bethlehem heaven sympathized with earth. A wave of joy dashed clear over the battlements and dripped upon the shepherds in the words: "Glory to God in the highest, and on earth peace, good will toward men." In my next sentence every word weighs a ton. "God so loved the world that he gave his only begotten Son, that whosoever believeth in him should not perish, but have everlasting life." Show me any other book with such a doctrine—so high, so deep, so vast.

The Bible Is Right in Its Effects

I do not care where you put the Bible, it just suits the place. You put it in the hand of a man seriously concerned about his soul. I see people often giving to the serious soul this and that book. It may be very well; but there is no book like the Bible. He reads the commandments and pleads to the indictment: "Guilty." He takes up the Psalms of David and says: "They just describe my feelings." He flies to good works. Paul starts him out of that by the announcement: "A man is not justified by works." He falls back in his discouragement. The Bible starts him up with the sentence: "Remember Lot's wife. Grieve not the Spirit. Flee the wrath to come." Then the man, in despair, begins to cry out: "What shall I do? Where shall

I go?" And a voice reaches him, saying: "Come to me, all ye who are weary and heavy laden, and I will give you rest." Take this Bible and place it in the hands of men in trouble. Is there anybody here in trouble? Ah! I might better ask, Are there any here who have never been in trouble? Put this Bible in the hands of the troubled.

You find that as some of the best berries grow on the sharpest thorns, so some of the sweetest consolations of the Gospel grow on the most stinging afflictions. You thought that death had grasped your child. Oh, no. It was only the heavenly Shepherd taking a lamb out of the cold. Christ bent over you as you held the child in your lap and putting His arms gently around the little one said, "Of such is the kingdom of heaven." Put the Bible in the school. Palsied be the hand that would take the Bible from the college and the school. Educate only a man's head and you make him an infidel. Educate only a man's heart and you make him a fanatic. Educate them both together and you have the noblest work of God. An educated mind without moral principles is a ship without a helm, a rushing train without brakes, or reversing rod to control the speed. Put the Bible in the family. There it lies on the table, an unlimited power. Polygamy and unscriptural divorce are prohibited. Parents are kind and faithful, children polite and obedient. Domestic sorrows lessened by being divided, joys increased by being multiplied. Oh, father, oh, mother, take down that long neglected Bible and read it yourselves, and let your children read it. Put the Bible on the train and on shipboard until all parts of this land and all other lands shall have its illumination. This hour there rises the yell of heathen worship and in the face of this day's sun smokes the blood of human sacrifice. Give them the Bible. Unbind that wife from the funeral pyre, for no other sacrifice is needed, since the blood of Jesus Christ cleanses from all sin.

I am preaching this sermon because there are so many who would have you believe that the Bible is an outlandish Book and obsolete. It is fresher and more intense than any book that yesterday came out of your great publishing houses. Make it your guide in life and your pillow in death.

After the battle of Richmond, a dead soldier was found with his hand lying on an open Bible. The summer insects had eaten the flesh from the hand, but the skeleton finger lay on these words: "Yea, though I walk through the valley of the shadow of death, I will fear no evil; for thou art with me, thy rod and thy staff they comfort me." Yes, this Book will become in your last days, when you turn away from all other books, a solace for your soul. Perhaps it will be your mother's Bible, perhaps the one given you on your wedding day, its cover now worn out and leaves faded with age. But its bright promises will flash upon the opening gates of heaven.

> How precious is the Book divine
>   By inspiration given;
> Bright as a lamp its doctrines shine
>   To guide our souls to heaven.

> This lamp, through all the tedious night
>   Of life shall guide our way,
> Till we behold the clearer light
>   Of an eternal day.

The Sanctifying Power of the Word

Wilbur Moorhead Smith (1894–1977) was born in Chicago where his father had been converted to Christ under the ministry of D. L. Moody. Educated at Moody Bible Institute and the College of Wooster, Wilbur Smith was soon recognized as an omnivorous reader and incurable bibliophile. From 1913 to 1937, he pastored Presbyterian churches in Maryland, Virginia, and Pennsylvania; and in 1938 became Professor of English Bible at Moody Bible Institute. His encyclopedic knowledge of books and authors was shared not only in the classroom, but also in numerous magazine articles and radio addresses. From 1947 to 1963, he taught at Fuller Seminary, and from 1963 to 1971, at Trinity Evangelical Divinity School, Deerfield, Illinois.

This sermon was the third of five messages Dr. Smith gave at the British Keswick Conference in 1952, all of which were published by Zondervan as *The Word of God and the Life of Holiness*.

Wilbur Moorhead Smith

6

THE SANCTIFYING POWER OF THE WORD

Sanctify them through thy truth: thy word is truth (John 17:17).

WE ARE THINKING together of the place of the Word of God in the life of holiness. Let us consider a word from the lips of our Lord on the sanctifying power of the Word of God from His high priestly prayer in John 17.

This is the only place in which Christ ever spoke of sanctification. He did say that the Temple sanctifies the gift, and so on, but in relation to men and women this is the only time that He ever actually used the word. He used it in a prayer—His last great prayer to His Father for us: "Sanctify them through thy truth: thy word is truth" (John 17:17). In the passage, "Be ye holy for I am holy, saith the Lord," the Greek word for "holy" is the adjective of which this word "sanctify" is the verb. So we can really say that our Lord prayed: "Make them holy in thy truth: thy word is truth."

Now I must confess that I have never seen anything on this text that satisfies me. I went through all the Keswick volumes from 1875, looking for anything pertaining to my subject. While there were in the early days perhaps two messages on this text, the speakers did what some preachers do—took the text and then went into all the world preaching the Gospel! I do not want to do that. But I want to give this text very careful examination. I would not do so if this were a line from Plato or Aristotle or Virgil. But this is a sentence from the One who has redeemed us, from the One whose name we bear, by whose blood we are cleansed, in whose image we are being continually made, and who will bring us home to God in glory. This is the One of whom it is said in John

10:36 that He had been sanctified by the Father. This is the prayer of our Lord to the Father that we should be sanctified in the truth: "Thy word is truth."

We will consider three things on the sanctifying power of the Word. First, we will consider *the meaning of being sanctified, or holy.* Second, we will look at *the need for separation or sanctification.* And, finally, we will *come to the means of sanctification.*

The Meaning of Sanctification

In the Old Testament the Hebrew word translated "to sanctify" means "to cut off" or "to separate," and thus to dedicate for a solemn purpose. Turn to Leviticus 27 just to get an understanding of this word because we can be so vague on this matter of sanctification. Some think it means we are to give up tobacco and drink and to eliminate the movies. Others think it means to have some hysterics, to be pious, or something of that sort.

> And when a man shall sanctify his house to be holy unto the Lord, then the priest shall estimate it, whether it be good or bad. . . . And if a man shall sanctify unto the Lord some part of a field of his possession. . . . But if he sanctify his field after the jubile. . . . Only the firstling of the beasts, which should be the Lord's firstling, no man shall sanctify it; whether it be ox, or sheep: it is the Lord's. . . . Notwithstanding no devoted thing ["devoted" means to give up] that a man shall devote unto the Lord of all that he hath, both of man and beast, and of the field of his possession, shall be sold or redeemed: every devoted thing is most holy unto the Lord (vv. 14–28).

This means to dedicate or separate a house, a field, a beast, and last, to separate men to the Lord. That is the first meaning—it belongs to Him. Then that which was common—a field was common, a house was just an ordinary house, the beast was just an ordinary beast—and is then devoted and yielded to God, as a man or a woman, partakes of a new life. One partakes of that to which the man or woman is dedicated. That is, he is not only separate, but he is living a new kind of life.

First Peter 2:9–10 gives a definition.

> But ye are a chosen generation, a royal priesthood, an holy nation, a peculiar people [separate]; that ye should shew forth [which we never did before] the praises of him who hath called you out of darkness into his marvellous light; which in time past were not a people, but are now the people of God.

This is not the lesson today, but the passage goes on:

> I beseech you as strangers and pilgrims [separated to God], abstain from fleshly lusts, which war against the soul (v. 11).

We are separated first, then we partake of a new life. We belong to God, then we are to live for God.

Let me give a definition from the great Dutch theologian, Bavinck, which is as good as anything I have seen: "Sanctification is setting apart, and something more. It means that by washing, by sacrifice, by sprinkling with blood, a thing loses its common character (a thing or a man loses its common character—which it possessed in common with other things or men), and has been given a new character, so that it now lives in this new condition."

Not only are we separate—that is, positional—but there is also something experimental here. We have the basis for this word in the prayer of our Lord Jesus: "Sanctify them through thy truth: thy word is truth."

The Need for Sanctification

Now let us look at the second point of this brief sentence, and that is *the need for separation or sanctification*. We will find this in John 17:11–12: "I am no more in the world, but these are in the world, and I come to thee. Holy Father, keep through thine own name those whom thou hast given me, that they may be one, even as we are. While I was with them in the world, I kept them in thy name. . . and [I guarded them]." Whether we recognize it or not, we need divine protection. These two words, "keep" and "guard," mean a divine Father's watchful care. What do you guard? You guard your jewels, if you have any left after the income tax is paid. You guard your barns, your homes, your precious little children. You do not set a guard over the dirt in the backyard—you can get some more—because that is common. You do not set a guard over a few bricks or a couple of flowers on the front lawn. You will not sit up all night to watch them. You guard what is precious and what is in danger of being stolen or taken away.

I am not talking about salvation. God keeps guard of His own and not one shall perish. Our Lord went on to pray: "I have given them thy word; and the world hath hated them, because they are not of the world [—you and me—] even as I am not of the world" (v. 14). We are still here in the world. Sometimes we wish we were not. But He said, "I pray not that thou shouldest take them out of the world, but that thou shouldest keep them from the evil. . . . As thou hast sent me into the world, even so I also sent them into the world" (vv. 15–18).

We have two enemies of our souls—the world and the Devil. Both of them would attack us. Both of them would drag us into their environment, into their principles, into their way of living, into their sinfulness. We are in the world, and whether we are aware of it or not, the Lord said you and I need protection from the world and from the Devil. He talks about it to the Father more than He talks about any other thing. He talks about His own in the world: "They hated me, and will hate them; I pray that Thou wilt keep them" Then He says, "Sanctify them through thy truth: thy word is truth."

What does that mean? I should have thought He would have said, "Sanctify them in holy living" not "in the truth." Turn to another passage to get the meaning of this, "If God were your Father, ye would love me: for I proceeded forth and came from God; neither came I of myself, but he sent me. Why do ye not understand my speech? even because ye cannot hear my word" (John 8:42–43). Then this, an awful sentence: "Ye are of your father the devil [the evil one; put a "d" in the front of "evil" and you have "devil"], and the lusts of your father ye will do. He was a murderer from the beginning, and he abode not in the truth, because there is no truth in him. When he speaketh a lie, he speaketh of his own: he is a liar, and the father of it" (v. 44).

I cannot read these awful words without being reminded of something I heard over thirty years ago. I heard Dr. Griffith Thomas speaking in Philadelphia on the work of Satan. I remember his prayer before those two thousand people, that the Devil himself might not paralyze his tongue as he came to expose the works of the evil one.

"And because I tell you the truth, ye believe me not. . . . If I say the truth, why do ye not believe me?" (vv. 45–46). That is one of the greatest questions of all time. "He that is of God heareth God's words: ye therefore hear them not, because ye are not of God" (v. 47).

"I pray . . . that thou shouldest keep them from the evil." "He abode not in the truth. . . . he is a liar, and the father of it." How are we to be kept from the liar who is the father of lies? We can only be kept from him by the truth. And faced with delusion and diabolical strategy, how are we to be delivered from the errors of the wicked one except by the truth of God? Now, we are marked off. We belong to the Lord Jesus. Christ, aware of the allurement and fascination and pressure and power of the world and of Satan, said to the Father, "Sanctify them through thy truth: thy word is truth."

I want to lay stress on this need. In Revelation 12:9 there is a phrase that has come upon me with new and awful significance in the last few weeks. Satan is given four titles, and then he is called "[the deceiver] of the whole world." This means even of Oxford and Cambridge, and Harvard and Yale, and the Sorbonne. This means wicked men and wise men: "[He] deceiveth the whole world."

I do not know about your vocabulary here, but I am

sure it is the same as with us. In the last two years only have you had this ghastly phrase, "The big lie." The *New York Times* had a frightening editorial recently called "The Lie in Action." It was referring to a demonstration in Paris when General Ridgeway was visiting that city. I am not defending the General, or my country, or anything else. But the demonstrators had a big placard bearing the words, "Ridgeway, Microbe Killer." They knew that this was a lie. The *New York Times* observed what a terrible age this is when men will go out in the streets and fight not for something they believe in, even though they know it to be wrong, but *for what they know to be a lie*.

This is exactly what the apostle Paul meant in 2 Thessalonians when he said the Lord would send a spirit of delusion upon those who love not the truth, and they would believe a lie. I do not know if it troubles you, but it troubles me. We talk about "resting in the Word." I hope I can rest in the Word, too. But I would like to know today why one billion people in thirty years come under the power of an atheistic communism, and only a few trickle into the kingdom of our Lord Jesus Christ and to the Gospel of truth. I wonder why? I do not want anyone to say to me it is the Devil, because I have a Lord who is greater than the Devil. He is Sovereign and Lord. It is a mystery to me why millions and millions believe a lie and only so few are coming into the truth in Christ. Now with millions coming under this delusion, if ever in the Christian church we needed this message we need it today: "Sanctify My people—separate them from this spirit of the world."

The Means of Sanctification

We have seen the meaning of it and the need of it, now *the means*. "Sanctify them through thy truth; thy word is truth." In John 17:8 our Lord says, "I have given unto them the words which thou gavest me." I wonder when He received these words? "And they have received them, and have known surely that I came out from thee, and they believed that thou didst send me. . . . I have given them thy word" (vv. 8–14). So the Word of God is com-municated to us through the Lord Jesus. "Sanctify them through thy truth; thy word is truth."

Now you have about six times in the Scriptures this phrase: "the word of truth" (Ps. 119:43; 2 Cor. 6:7; Eph. 1:13; Col. 1:5; 2 Tim. 2:15; James 1:18). "Thy word is truth," "the word of truth." I ask you, the truth about what? Here one could spend hours. I think the first car-dinal fact is the truth concerning the Lord Jesus, and concerning His Father and the Holy Spirit.

About two years ago my wife and I were in a lovely town in northern California called Carmel-by-the-sea—a place for artists and musicians beside the ocean, and with very nice country in which we could be quiet. It is rather pagan, but not wicked. During the week I saw some posters with the title of a lecture, "Christian Science, the Fulfillment of Prophecy and Promise." Now, I said to myself, That is my field—prophecy. And I have just forgotten what prophecy there is concerning Christian Science. I could name a couple, but they were not in their minds! So I went to hear this lecture. There were about five hundred people present. They were the nicest-looking people you ever saw, and as intelligent as any audience you will ever face in America. The man lectured for an hour. He said that the promise of Jesus that He would send the Comforter, the Holy Spirit, was fulfilled in the coming of Mary Baker Eddy. He also stated that Christian Science is the Third Person of the Godhead. He said that when the Lord told the parable of the woman sweeping the house and finding the lost coin, He was speaking of Mary Baker Eddy sweeping the church of dogma and finding the truth, which was Christian Science. He took up about eight New Testament passages. He was quoting the Bible and made it tell what it did not tell. He said that this man Jesus had to put us all on the same level.

What I am getting at is, that when you get into that area and believe that, you are no longer separated to God the Father of our Lord Jesus Christ. "Sanctify them through thy truth: thy word is truth." And in this day, when there are so many compromises and a weakening of our Christian faith and a loss of confidence in the Word of God, beloved, there never was a time when it was more necessary to draw the line of demarcation and speak out the truth that separated us to God.

Let me give another illustration from one of our own professors. I have quoted this before. He wrote me a letter recently and said, "It is so hard to express oneself; I find difficulty." He has three doctorate degrees, and by that time he ought to be able to express himself! He is Professor of World Religion—whatever that might be—at one of our universities that has fourteen thousand students. He said, "A large part of the educational path today within the Christian fold is to guide people in such a way that they no longer feel it necessary to read the Christian Scriptures." You teach that to fourteen thousand young people and you are going to have trouble on your hands!

In a day like this, we need to saturate ourselves more with the Word of God than we ever have in our lives. This is the time when our ears must be open to the Word of God. "Sanctify them through thy truth: thy word is truth."

The reason we need this Word is because our experiences can pass away, and the teaching of men can lose its significance, and times can change. But, beloved, this is the norm: "Thy word is settled in heaven" (Ps. 119:89). H. G. Wells, Bob Ingersoll, and Thomas Paine cried for a new Bible. They never had one, and there will not be one. There is only one revealed Word of God, and this is it. When our Lord was on His knees about to go to Calvary, He cried to the Father to "sanctify them through thy truth: thy word is truth." If we belong to God, we need God's truth. If we are to be separated to God, we need God's Word. There is no policy, no music and no art, nor any ritual in the world that can ever be a substitute for the Word of God. "Sanctify them through thy truth: thy word is truth."

We are losing our contact with this Book, and we must get back to it. In the old days the Methodists took two books to church, the Bible and the hymnbook. Now the Methodists take one book, the hymnbook.

I think a lot of people are doing what I heard Robert Lee talk about one time. He was our great southern orator and President of the World Baptist Association. He said that when he was a young minister he was itinerating in the mountains of Tennessee, and one night he had to stop at a log cabin where there were twelve children. After supper he said, "Before we go to bed we should have family prayer and read the Bible. Will you get a Bible?" The mother said, "Sonny, go out in the living room and get the Bible." The boy returned and said, "Mother, it is not there." "Sylvia, go upstairs to the bedroom and bring down the Bible." And again the reply came, "It is not there." "That is funny. Where is the Bible?" After several of the children had sought in different directions, one chipped in with a word of knowledge and said, "It is in the toolbox in the wood shed." And the Bible was found there, along with liniments and things used for beasts and lambs.

The Book that could save their souls and that came from God was in the woodshed in a toolbox. That is what modern man is doing with the Word of God—and some Christians, too. We are keeping this Book closed or locked in a woodshed or some other place. Without it we shall not have the sanctified life that we need for this desperate age.

Dr. Robert Speer some years ago was going to China as the head of our Foreign Missions' Board. He was discussing something with the young ministers and said to one, "Would you mind bringing up your Bible from the state room?" And the young man said, "I am sorry, but we are not supposed to have much luggage in the state room, so I left my Bible in the baggage in the hold." Robert Speer said, "Young man, I am the General Secretary of the Presbyterian Board of Foreign Missions. If the Bible means no more to you than that, the first ship to go home from China is the ship you are going to take." If that man needed that Bible in China, beloved, we need it in London, Liverpool, and New York: "Sanctify them through thy truth: thy word is truth."

This probably has not yet come to you, but it has come to our country. And I am shocked and disturbed. In a lot of churches—some famous and with great traditions—I am discovering with great alarm that the Sunday morning program when it is handed to me includes an invocation, two anthems, *Te Deums,* and an offering, but no place for the reading of the Word of God. I always say, "We will have a place for the Word of God. If the sermon is no good, the Word of God will be." "Sanctify them through thy truth: thy word is truth."

Look again at John 17:19, "And for their sakes"— that is, for you and me—"I sanctify myself, that they also may be sanctified through the truth." "For their sakes . . ."; that they may be. . ."—you can put any word in there you want. Just what are you going to be? The Lord said, "I sanctify myself, that they also may be sanctified." You and I are going to have a tremendous influence over the sanctified or unsanctified lives of other people. People will draw from us the inspiration of this hour. They are never going to be lifted any higher than you and I are lifted. "For their sakes"—in order that they may be sanctified—"I sanctify myself."

What did one of the speakers say about Bishop Taylor Smith, "of blessed memory"? Then he supported some arguments by giving details of his wonderful life. Bishop Taylor Smith has been dead some years, and the influence of his holy life is still here. That is a wonderful way to live. Of course, you know the story of his early days when he got saved. It took all night, but he dedicated every single part of his whole body to God forever. He told this to a friend of mine: "I even asked the Lord for a holy voice, and He gave it to me." I will tell you what I heard in America. He was at dinner in the home of Dr. Houghton, the President of the Moody Bible Institute, and about twelve of us were there. When the bishop left, a friend said to me, "I feel as though I had been in the presence of the Lord Jesus." What a way to live! "Sanctify them through thy truth: thy word is truth." "And for their sakes I sanctify myself, that they also may be sanctified through the truth."

NOTES

Ten Reasons Why I Believe the Bible Is the Word of God

Reuben Archer Torrey (1856–1928) was one of America's best-known evangelists and Bible teachers. Educated at Yale and various German universities, he went through a time of skepticism from which he emerged a staunch preacher of the faith. In 1889, D. L. Moody called Torrey from the pastorate to become superintendent of his new school in Chicago, now the Moody Bible Institute. He also served as pastor of the Chicago Avenue Church, now the Moody Church. He and Charles Alexander conducted evangelistic meetings together in many parts of the world. From 1912–1919, Torrey served as dean of the Bible Institute of Los Angeles. He served from 1914 as pastor of the Church of the Open Door. From 1924 to his death, he ministered in conferences and taught at the Moody Bible Institute.

This sermon was taken from volume 3 of the "Great Pulpit Masters" series, published in 1950 by Fleming H. Revell.

Reuben Archer Torrey

7

TEN REASONS WHY I BELIEVE THE BIBLE IS THE WORD OF GOD

Thy word is a lamp unto my feet, and a light unto my path (Psalm 119:105).

SOME FIFTEEN or sixteen years ago, when a student in Yale Theological Seminary, I was first confronted seriously with the question: Why do you believe the Bible is the Word of God? Doubtless the question had often floated vaguely through my mind before, but now it stood out definitely, vividly, and persistently. It was the one all-absorbing thought that engaged my mind by day and by night. I had doubtless many friends who could have answered the question satisfactorily. But I was unwilling to confide to them the struggle that was going on in my heart, so I sought help from God and from books. After much painful study and thought, I came out of the darkness of skepticism into the broad daylight of faith and certainty that the Bible from beginning to end is God's Word. The address which Mr. Moody has asked me to deliver tonight is the outcome of that experience. My subject is, "Why I believe the Bible is the Word of God."

The Testimony of Jesus Christ

First, I believe the Bible is the Word of God *from the testimony of Jesus Christ*. Many people accept the authority of Christ who do not accept that of the Bible as a whole. We all must accept His authority. He is accredited to us by five divine things: (1) by the divine life He lived; (2) by the divine words He spoke; (3) by the divine works He wrought; (4) by the divine attestation of the resurrection from the dead; and (5) by His divine influence on the history of mankind. But if we accept the authority of Christ, we must accept the authority of the

Bible as a whole. He testifies definitely and specifically to the divine authorship of the whole Bible. We find His testimony as to the Old Testament in Mark 7:13. Here He calls the law of Moses the "Word of God." That, of course, covers only the first five books of the Old Testament. But in Luke 24:27 we read, "And beginning at Moses and all the prophets, he expounded unto them in *all the scriptures* the things concerning himself." And in verse 44 He says, "All things must be fulfilled which were written in the law of Moses, and in the prophets, and in the psalms."

The Jews, as most of you know, divided the Old Testament into three parts—the Law, the Prophets, and the Psalms—and Christ takes up each of these parts and sets the stamp of His authority on it. In John 10:35 Christ says, "The scripture cannot be broken," thereby teaching the absolute accuracy and inviolability of the Old Testament. More specifically still, if possible, in Matthew 5:18 Jesus says, "One jot or one tittle shall in no wise pass from the law, till all be fulfilled." A jot is the smallest letter in the Hebrew alphabet, less then half the size of any other letter. A tittle is the nearest point of a consonant, less than the cross we put on a "t." Christ here tells them the Scripture is absolutely true, down to the smallest letter or point of a letter. So if we accept the authority of Christ we must accept the divine authority of the entire Old Testament.

Now, as to the New Testament. We find Christ's endorsement of it in John 14:26: "The Holy Ghost, whom the Father will send in my name, he shall teach you all things, and bring all things to your remembrance, whatsoever I have said unto you." Here we see that not only was the teaching of the apostles to be fully inspired, but also their recollection of what Christ Himself taught. We are sometimes asked how we know that the apostles correctly reported what Jesus said. They may have forgotten. True, they might forget. But Christ Himself tells us that in the Gospel we have not the apostles' recollection of what He said, but the Holy Ghost's recollection—and the Spirit of God never forgets.

In John 16:13–14, Christ said that the Holy Ghost should guide the apostles into "all truth." Therefore in the New Testament teaching we have the whole sphere of God's truth. The teaching of the apostles is more complete than that of Jesus Himself, for He says in John 16:12–13, "I have yet many things to say unto you, but ye cannot bear them now. Howbeit, when he, the Spirit of truth, is come, he shall guide you into all truth." While His own teaching had been partial because of their weakness, the teaching of the apostles under the promised Spirit was to take in the whole sphere of God's truth. So if we accept the authority of Christ we must accept that of the whole Bible. But we must, as already seen, accept Christ's authority.

The Bible's Fulfilled Prophecies

Second, I believe the Bible is the Word of God *from its fulfilled prophecies*. There are two classes of prophecies in the Bible: first, the explicit, verbal prophecies; second, those of the types. In the first we have the definite prophecies concerning the Jews, the heathen nations, and the Messiah. Taking the prophecies regarding the Messiah as an illustration, look at Isaiah 53; Micah 5:2; Daniel 9:25–27. Many others might be mentioned, but these will serve as illustrations. In these prophecies, written hundreds of years before the Messiah came, we have the most explicit statement as to the manner and place of His birth, His reception by men, how His life would end, His resurrection, and His victory following His death. When made, these prophecies were exceedingly improbable and seemingly impossible of fulfillment, but they were fulfilled to the very minutest detail of manner and place and time.

How are we to account for it? Man could not have foreseen these improbable events—they lay hundreds of years ahead—but God could. It is God who speaks through these men. But the prophecies of the types are more remarkable still. Everything in the Old Testament—history, institutions, ceremonies—is prophetic. The high priesthood, the ordinary priesthood, the

Levites, the prophets, the priests, and the kings are all prophecies. The tabernacle, the brazen altar, the laver, the golden candlestick, the table of showbread, the veil, the altar of incense, the ark of the covenant, the very coverings of the tabernacle are prophecies. In all these things—as we study them minutely and soberly in the light of the history of Jesus Christ and the church—we see wrapped up in the ancient institutions, ordained of God to meet an immediate purpose, prophecies of the death and atonement and resurrection of Christ, the day of Pentecost, and the entire history of the church. We see the profoundest Christian doctrines of the New Testament clearly foreshadowed in these institutions of the Old Testament.

The only way in which you can appreciate it is to get into the Book itself and study all about the sacrifices and feasts, etc., until you see the truths of the New Testament shining out in the Old. If, in studying some elementary form of life, I find a rudimentary organ that is useless now but by the process of development is to become of use in that animal's descendant, I say that back of this rudimentary organ is God, who—in the earlier animal—is preparing for the life and necessities of the animal that is to come. So, going back to those preparations in the Bible for the truth that is to be clearly taught at a later day, there is only one scientific way to account for them: namely, He who knows and prepares for the end from the beginning is the author of that Book.

The Unity of the Bible

Third, I believe the Bible is the Word of God *from the unity of the Book*. This is an old argument, but a very satisfactory one. The Bible consists, as you know, of sixty-six books written by more than thirty different men, extending—in the period of its composition—over more than fifteen hundred years. It was written in four different languages, in many different countries. It was written by men on every plane of social life, from the herdsman and fisherman and cheap politician, to the king on his throne. And it was written under all sorts of circumstances. Yet in all this wonderful conglomeration we find an absolute unity of thought. The wonderful thing about it is that this unity does not lie on the surface. On the surface there is oftentimes apparent contradiction. The unity comes out only after deep and protracted study. More wonderful yet is the organic character of this unity, beginning in the first book and growing until you come to its culmination in the last book of the Bible. We have first the seed, then the plant, then the bud, then the blossom, then the ripened fruit.

Suppose a vast building had been erected, the stones for which were brought from the quarries in Rutland, Vermont; Berea, Ohio; Kasota, Minnesota; and Middletown, Connecticut. Each stone was hewn into shape in the quarry from which it was brought. These stones were of all varieties of shape and size—cubical, rectangular, cylindrical, etc. But when they were brought together every stone fit in its place. When put together there rose before you a temple absolutely perfect in every outline—with its domes, side walls, buttresses, arches, transepts—not a gap or a flaw anywhere. How would you account for it? You would say that back of these individual workers in the quarries was the master mind of the architect who planned it all. So in this marvelous temple of God's truth that we call the Bible— whose stones have been quarried at periods of time and in places so remote from one another but where every smallest part fits each other part—we are forced to say that back of the human hands that wrought was the Master mind that thought.

The Immeasurable Superiority of the Bible's Teachings

Fourth, I believe the Bible is the Word of God *from the immeasurable superiority of the teachings of the Bible to those of any other and all other books*. It was very fashionable five or ten years ago to compare the teachings of the Bible with the teachings of Zoroaster, Buddha, Confucius, Epictetus, Socrates, Marcus Aurelius Antoninus, and a number of other heathen authors. The difference between the teachings of the Bible and those of these men is found in three points. First, the Bible has in it *nothing but* truth, while all the others have truth mixed with error. It is true Socrates taught how a philosopher ought to die. He also taught how a woman of the town ought to conduct her business. Jewels there are in the teachings of these men. But, as Joseph Cook said, they are jewels picked out of the mud.

Second, the Bible contains *all* truth. There is not a truth to be found anywhere on moral or spiritual subjects that you cannot find, in substance, within the covers of that old Book. I have often, when speaking on this subject, asked anyone to bring me a single truth on moral or spiritual subjects which, on reflection, I could not find within the covers of this Book. No one has ever been able to do it. I took pains to compare some of the better teachings of Ingersoll with those of the Bible. Ingersoll indeed has jewels of thought, but they were—whether he knew it or not—stolen jewels, and stolen from the very Book he ridiculed.

The third point of superiority is this: The Bible contains *more* truth than all other books together. Get together from all literature of ancient and modern times all the beautiful thoughts you can. Put away all the rubbish. Then put all these truths that you have culled from the literature of all ages into one book. As the result, even then you will not have a book that will take the place of this one Book. This is not a large Book. I hold in my hand a copy that I carry in my vest pocket, and yet in this one little Book there is more of truth than in all the books that man has produced in all the ages of his history. How will you account for it? There is only one rational way. This is not man's book but God's Book.

The Bible's History and Victory Over Attack

Fifth, I believe the Bible is the Word of God *from the history of the Book, and from its victory over attack*. This Book has always been hated. No sooner was this Book given to the world than it met the hatred of men, and they tried to stamp it out. Celsus tried it by the brilliancy of his genius, Porphyry by the depth of his philosophy, but they failed. Lucien directed against it the shafts of his ridicule, Diocletian, the power of the Roman empire, but they failed. Edicts backed by all the power of the empire were issued that every Bible should be burned and that everyone who had a Bible should be put to death. For eighteen centuries every engine of destruction that human science, philosophy, wit, reasoning, or brutality could bring to bear upon a book has been brought to bear upon that Book to stamp it out of the world. But it has a mightier hold on the world today than ever before. If that were man's book, it would have been annihilated and forgotten hundreds of years ago. But because there is in it "the hiding of [God's] power" (Hab. 3:4)—though at times all the great men of the world have been against it and only an obscure remnant for it. Still it has fulfilled wonderfully the words of Christ, though not in the sense of the original prophecy: "Heaven and earth shall pass away, but my word shall not pass away."

The Character of Those Who
Accept and Reject the Bible

Sixth, I believe the Bible is the Word of God *from the character of those who accept and those who reject the Book*. Two things speak for the divinity of the Bible: the character of those who accept it, and, equally, the character of those who reject it. I do not mean by that that every man who professes to believe the Book is better than every man that does not. But show me a man living an unselfish, devoted life who, without reservation, has surrendered himself to do the will of God, and I will show you a man who believes the Bible to be God's Word. On the other hand, show me a man who rejects the divine authority of that Book, and I will show you a man living a life of greed or lust or spiritual pride or self-will.

Suppose you had a book purporting to be by a certain author. The people best acquainted with that author say it is his, and the people least acquainted with him say it is not. Which would you believe? Now, the people best acquainted with God say the Bible is His Book; those who are least acquainted with God say it is not. Which will you believe? Furthermore, as men grow better, they are more likely to accept the Bible. As they grow worse, they are more likely to reject it. We have all known men who were both sinful and unbelieving, who by forsaking their sin lost their unbelief. Did any of us ever know a man who was sinful and believing, who by forsaking his sin lost his faith? The nearer men live to God, the more confident they are that the Bible is God's Word. The farther they get away from Him, the more confident they are that it is not.

Where is the stronghold of the Bible? In the pure, unselfish, happy home. Where is the stronghold of infidelity? The gambling hall, the drinking saloon, and the brothel. If a man should walk into a saloon, lay a Bible down on the bar, and order a drink, we should think there a strange incongruity in his actions. But if he should lay a work on Colonel Ingersoll, or any infidel writing, on the bar and order a drink, we would not feel that there was any incongruity.

The Bible's Influence

Seventh, I believe the Bible is the Word of God *from the influence of the Book*. There is more power in that little Book to save men, and purify, gladden, and beautify their lives, than in all other literature put together. There is more power in the Bible to lift men up to God. A stream never rises higher than its source. A book that has a power to lift men up to God that no other book has, must have come down from God in a way that no other book has. I have in mind as I speak a man who was the most complete victim of strong drink I ever knew. He was a man of marvelous intellectual gifts, but who had been stupefied and brutalized and demonized by the power of sin. He was an infidel. At last, the light of God shone into his darkened heart. By the power of that Book he has been transformed into one of the humblest, sweetest, noblest men I know today. What other book would have done that? What other book has the power to elevate not only individuals, but communities and nations that this Book has?

The Bible's Inexhaustible Depth

Eighth, I believe the Bible is the Word of God *from the inexhaustible depth of the Book*. Nothing has been added to it in eighteen hundred years, yet a man like Bunsen or Neander cannot exhaust it by the study of a lifetime. George Muller has read it through more than one hundred times and says it is fresher every time he reads it. Could that be true of any other book? But more wonderful than this—not only individual men but generations of men for eighteen hundred years have dug into it and given to the world thousands of volumes devoted to its exposition, and they have not reached the bottom of the quarry yet. A book that man produces man can exhaust. But all men together have not been able to get to the bottom of this Book. How are you going to account for it? Only in this way—that in this Book are hidden the infinite and inexhaustible treasures of the wisdom and knowledge of God. A Unitarian writer, in trying to disprove the inspiration of the Bible, says, "How irreligious to charge an infinite God with having written His whole Word in so small a book." He does not see how his argument can be turned against himself. What a testimony it is to the divinity of this Book that such infinite wisdom is stored away in so small a compass.

As We Grow in Knowledge and Holiness, We Grow Toward the Bible

Ninth, I believe the Bible is the Word of God *from the fact that as we grow in knowledge and holiness, we grow toward the Bible*. Every thoughtful person here, when he started out to study the Bible, found many things with which he did not agree. But as he went on studying and growing in likeness to God, the nearer he got to God and the nearer he got to the Bible. The nearer and nearer we get to God's standpoint, the less and less becomes the disagreement between us and the Bible. What is the inevitable mathematical conclusion? When we get where God is, we and the Bible will meet. In other words, the Bible was written from God's standpoint.

Suppose you are traveling through a forest under conduct of an experienced and highly recommended guide. You come to a place where two roads diverge. The guide says the road to the left is the one to take, but your own judgment—passing on the facts before it—sees clear evidence that the road to the right is the one to take. You turn and say to the guide, "I know you have had large experience in this forest, and you have come to me highly recommended. But my own judgment tells me clearly that the road to the right is the one we should take, and I must follow my own judgment." But after you have gone on that path for some distance you are obliged to stop, turn around and go back and take the path which the guide said was the right one. After awhile you come to another place where two roads diverge. Now the guide says the road to the right is the one to take, but your own judgment clearly says the one to the left is the one to take. Again you follow your own judgment, with the same result as before. After you had had this experience forty or fifty times and found yourself wrong every time, I think you would have sense enough the next time to follow the guide.

That is just my experience with the Bible. Like almost all other young men, my confidence became shaken. I came to the fork in the road more than forty times, and I followed my own reason. In the outcome I found myself wrong and the Bible right every time. I trust that from this time on I shall have sense enough to follow the teachings of the Bible, whatever my own judgment may say.

The Direct Testimony of the Holy Spirit

Tenth, I believe the Bible is the Word of God *from the direct testimony of the Holy Spirit*. We started with God and shall end with God. We started with the testimony of the Second Person of the Trinity and will close with that of the Third Person of the Trinity. The Holy Spirit sets His seal in the soul of every believer to the divine authority of the Bible. It is possible to get to a place where we need no argument to prove that the Bible is God's

Word. Christ says, "My sheep know my voice," and God's children know His voice. I know that the voice that speaks to me from the pages of that Book is the voice of my Father.

You will sometimes meet a pious old lady who will tell you that she knows that the Bible is God's Word. When you ask her for a reason for believing that it is God's Word, she can give you none. She simply says she knows it is God's Word. You say that is mere superstition. Not at all. She is one of Christ's sheep and distinguishes her Shepherd's voice from every other voice. She is one of God's children and knows that the voice that speaks to her from the Bible is the voice of God. She is above argument. Everyone can have that testimony. John 7:17 (RV) tells you how to get it. "If any man willeth to do his will, he shall know of the teaching, whether it be of God." Just surrender your will to the will of God, no matter where it carries you. You thus will put yourself in such an attitude toward God that when you read this Book you will recognize that the voice that speaks to you from it is the voice of the God to whom you have surrendered your will.

Some time ago, when I was speaking to our students on how to deal with skeptics, there was in the audience a graduate of Oxford University who had fallen into utter skepticism. At the close of the lecture he came to me and said, "I don't wish to be discourteous, sir, but my experience contradicts everything you have said." I asked him if he had followed the course of action that I had suggested and not found light. He said that he had. Stepping into another room, I had a pledge written out, running somewhat as follows:

> I believe there is an absolute difference between right and wrong, and I hereby take my stand upon the right, to follow it wherever it carries me. I promise to earnestly endeavor to find out what the truth is, and if I ever find that Jesus Christ is the Son of God, I promise to accept Him as my Savior and confess Him before the world.

I handed the paper to the gentleman and asked him if he was willing to sign it. He answered, "Certainly," and did sign it. I said to him, "You don't know there is not a God, and you don't know that God doesn't answer prayer. I know He does, but my knowledge cannot avail for you, but here is a possible clue to knowledge. Now you have promised to search earnestly for the truth, so you will follow this possible clue. I want you to offer a prayer like this: 'Oh, God, if there be any God and thou dost answer prayer, show me whether Jesus Christ is the Son, and if He is, I will accept Him as my Savior and confess Him before the world.'" This he agreed to do. I further requested that he would take the gospel of John and read in it every day, reading only a few verses at a time—slowly and thoughtfully—every time asking God before he read to give him light. This he also agreed to do. But he finished by saying, "There is nothing in it."

However, at the end of a short time I met him again, and he said to me, "There is something in that." I replied, "I knew that." Then he went on to say it seemed just as if he had been caught up by the Niagara river and had been carried along, and that before long he would be a shouting Methodist. A short time ago I met this gentleman again. He said to me that he could not understand how he had been so blind, how he had ever listened to the reasoning that he had, and that it seemed to him utterly foolish now. I replied that the Bible would explain it to him, that "the natural man receiveth not the things of the Spirit of God" (1 Cor. 2:14). But that now that he had put himself in the right attitude toward God and His truth, everything had been made plain. That man, who had assured me that he was "a very peculiar man" and that methods that influenced others would not influence him, by putting himself into the right attitude toward God came to a place where he received the direct testimony of the Holy Spirit that this Bible is God's Word. And anyone else can do the same.

NOTES

Inspiration, Not Private Interpretation

George H. Morrison (1866–1928) assisted the great Alexander Whyte in Edinburgh, pastored two churches, and then became pastor in 1902 of the distinguished Wellington Church on University Avenue in Glasgow, Scotland. His preaching drew great crowds; in fact, people had to line up an hour before the services to be sure to get seats in the large auditorium. Morrison was a master of imagination in preaching, yet his messages are solidly biblical.

From his many published volumes of sermons, I have chosen this message, found in *The Weaving of Glory,* published in 1904 by Hodder and Stoughton, London.

George H. Morrison

8

INSPIRATION, NOT PRIVATE INTERPRETATION

No prophecy of the scripture is of any private interpretation (2 Peter 1:20).

THERE ARE SOME texts with the words of which we have been familiar since our childhood, and yet we may never have seriously asked ourselves what is their true meaning. Their cadence lingers with us through the years, enriched with recollections of the sanctuary, associated in sweet and tender ways with the worship at the family altar. Yet it may be that all the time we have been misinterpreting the Word of God or reading into it a sense that was not there. Now this text that I have chosen is one, I think, that is often so misread. The words have a most familiar sound, but have we ever really thought what they imply? It is on that that I would like to dwell tonight, for the subject is one of very deep importance. Rightly understood, it ought to assist us greatly in our conception of what inspiration is.

What Is the Scriptural View of Inspiration?

Observe that prophecy is a very large term. You must not confuse it with the word prediction. As the priest was one who spoke *to* God, so was the prophet one who spoke *for* God. And so the word prophecy, in such a place as this, is practically equivalent to our Scripture, which is the revelation of God through man to us. Well then, our text is sometimes held to mean that you and I must not interpret Scripture privately. That is, we must not take the Word of God and wrest it to our peculiar circumstances. That that is a common mishandling of Scripture every one of us this evening knows. When men are in doubt about some action, they often seize on a text to quiet their conscience. And it is this taking of the large Word of God and using it for our own private interest that Peter is supposed to be here speaking of. Now that is a warning that is always timely and never antiquated nor out of place. It is possible now, as nineteen hundred years ago, to wrest the Scripture to our own destruction. Yet the whole tenor of the passage shows us that it was not *that* which was in the mind of Peter when he wrote, "No prophecy . . . is of any private interpretation."

Again, these words have been taken to mean that we must not isolate the separate words of Scripture. We must not divorce them from the general sense and give them a private meaning of their own. The word heresy, as many of you know, just means such a picking and selecting. A heretic was a man who, out of the whole broad truth, chose out for himself this portion or that portion. And all the evils that have followed heresy, and all the gains that heresy has wrought, have sprung from the false and often passionate emphasis that was laid on the part and not the whole. Now that also is an important truth, for we must never isolate the words of Scripture. We must never take this text or that and interpret it out of connection with the whole. Yet once again, studying our passage and looking to the general bearing of it, I think it is clear that *that* was not Peter's thought when he spoke about private interpretation.

What, then, did the apostle mean? Well, it is clear that he meant something of this nature. The interpretation he speaks of is not yours or mine—the interpretation he speaks of is the prophet's. The writers of Holy Scripture were not analysts; the writers of Holy Scripture were interpreters. Before them passed, as in some vision, the doings of God in providence and grace. And the prophet's work was to interpret these and to show their meaning and to convey their message so that men might be built up in their faith. Now what Peter teaches is that that interpretation was not in any sense the prophet's own. He looked at things and saw meaning in them, but it was not his own meaning that he saw. It was not natural insight that conducted him nor any genius to discern what mattered—all that would have been a private rendering, and a private rendering is not the Scripture. No prophecy is a prophet's own interpreting. It is not given by the will of man. It is the interpretation of events by something different from human genius. It is the interpretation of events by the inspiration of the Holy Spirit dwelling in men and using every faculty for the glory of God and the blessing of mankind.

Let me say in passing that this view of Scripture is common both to the Old and the New Testaments. I should never dream of building up the doctrine if it had no other warrant than this text. I need not dwell on the Old Testament, for the fact is too patent there to be disputed. "And the word of the Lord *came* to Joel"—that is the attitude of all the prophets. But it may be that you have never noticed how the New Testament adopts that attitude in regard to the testimony of the apostles to Jesus, and to His death and resurrection. Does it not seem a very simple thing to bear testimony to certain facts of history? Could not an honest man with a fair mind have borne witness to the Crucifixion? And yet the apostles, who from first to last were witnesses and nothing else than witnesses, are regarded as only fit for that by the indwelling of the Holy Spirit. The Spirit of truth who proceedeth from the Father—it is He who is to witness, said our Lord. And we are witnesses of these things, cries Peter in the Acts, *and so also is the Holy Spirit*. In other words, these men who wrote the Scriptures interpreted the facts, not privately, but through a Spirit given from the Father who was something other than their genius.

Now this view of Scripture inspiration, which I see not how any can gainsay, sets it apart at once *in kind* from inspiration of every other sort.

Think, first, of the inspiration of the historian. Now a true historian is not an analyst. He is something more than a mere chronicler. It is for him to show the connection of events and to estimate their importance by their pregnancy. If he does that feebly and confusedly, then we say he is a poor historian. If he does it in a large and illuminative way, we say he has a genius for history. Yet even when there is a genius for history and logical power and a grasp of facts, all that we expect in the historian is his personal interpretation of the past. That is why Robertson will treat of a period in a manner wholly different from Hume. That is why Lecky, handling the same facts, will give them a different complexion from Macaulay. They are inspired, if you care to call them so (using the word in a loose and general way), yet at their best and wisest all they give us is their private interpretation of the past.

Or think of the inspiration of the dramatist as we have it, for instance, in the plays of Shakespeare. We are wont to say that Shakespeare is inspired, and that in a broad sense is true. Well now, suppose you take a play of Shakespeare—take, for instance, the play of *Macbeth*. You say that that is an inspired play. I ask you what you mean by that? Well, there is only one thing you can mean—if your words have any significance at all—and what you mean is something of this kind. You mean that Shakespeare took the few facts of history that he found in the dusty pages of some chronicle, and he touched them with life, covered them with beauty, and filled them with passion and reality. And this he did with his *own* imagination, and with all the teeming wealth of his *own* brain, and with all the warmth and passion inextinguishable of his own private and peculiar heart. *Macbeth* and *Hamlet* came by the will of man. They are the triumph of individual genius. Their power is contained in this, that they *are* the rendering of one personality. Were they less private in their interpretation, they would never move us as they so profoundly do. They do not live because the facts are facts. They live because Shakespeare is Shakespeare.

Now, brethren, over against all that, there stands the inspiration of the Scripture. Unlike all history and every drama, no prophecy is of private interpretation. When a poet is most genuinely inspired, then is he most genuinely himself. When Wordsworth is at his finest and his purest, then is he most emphatically Wordsworth.

But what you are taught about Holy Scripture is that it came not by the will of man, but holy men of God spoke as they were moved by the Holy Spirit. Isaiah did not look at events, brood upon them, and say, "Now this is my interpretation of them." John did not look at the cross and at the grave, and say, "This is how it all appears to me." But they looked at everything under that light of God, which is only kindled by the Holy Spirit, and looking so, they saw and, seeing, wrote. Mark you, I do not suggest that they were passive—to say that were to misinterpret everything. Probably their powers were never so alive as when they were writing a gospel or an epistle. All I say is, and all that Scripture says is, that what you have in the Bible is not genius. It is something different from, and something more divine than, a private interpretation of events.

This fact, let me just say in passing, explains the wonderful unity of Scripture. A deepened sense of that great unity is one great gain of recent Bible study. Men used to argue, and not so long ago, that the Scripture was in arms against itself. They used to argue that John and Paul and Peter were always quietly attacking or criticizing each other. But I do not know one scholar of authority who would ever dream of saying that today; whatever we have lost in recent criticism, we have gained immensely in the sense of unity. Now, if there were ever writers of vigorous and independent personality, I think you may take it that these writers were the men who have given us the New Testament. If there were ever men who would have looked at facts in diverse or antagonistic ways, John and Paul and Peter were such men. In other words, had the Scripture that they wrote been their own personal interpretation, then almost certainly you would have found between them differences that were irreconcilable. And the very fact that these are never found, when they are handling the deep things of God, is a witness to an inspiration different in kind from that of genius. There is the freest play of personality—the writers are penmen and not pens. At the back of every chapter that they wrote is a rich and individual experience. Yet such is the deep and underlying unity in all that is essential to salvation, that the more we study the more we are convinced that the Scripture came not by the will of man. No prophecy is a private rendering. Had it been so we should have had many Bibles. We should have had a Bible of John, where everything was love, perhaps; and a Bible of Paul, where everything was righteousness. And the very fact that the Testament is *one,* when men so different were the writers of it, speaks of more than individual genius in all its interpretation of events.

Are There Features in Scripture That Corroborate This View?

Now if this be the scriptural view of inspiration, then we may proceed to ask another question. We may ask: Are there any features in the Scripture that help to corroborate this view? No prophecy is a private rendering. The Scripture came not by the will of man. Are there any features in the Word of God that would incline us to accept that as the truth? In other words, do we find in Holy Scripture what it is almost incredible that we should find, had the writers been consulting their own will? When a man is following his own bent, there are certain things that he avoids. There are aspects of things that from certain standpoints may be highly and naturally uncongenial. And if you find these very aspects dwelt on and expanded and enforced, then you may reasonably conclude that something else is active besides the writer's individual will. Now that is exactly what one finds in Scripture. And one finds it the more, the more one's knowledge grows. There is a certain curious want of correspondence between the message and the men who uttered it. And I shall close by touching upon that in one or two of its most salient features, that we may see how evident it is that Scripture came not by the will of man.

First, then, I note how often prophetic doctrine contradicts the bias of the will. If there is one thing clear in the prophets, it is this—that the truths they uttered were often uncongenial. Now men have spoken uncongenial truths sometimes under a compelling sense of duty. When every interest urged them to be silent, their conscience has compelled them to speak out. But you can never explain that old prophetic fire by saying that it was duty that impassioned it, for duty seemed to point the other way. The call of duty is the call of loyalty. The call of duty is the call of home. The call of duty is the call of patriotism when the enemy is marching on the gate. And yet how often these old prophetic heroes lifted the voice up in the name of God and contradicted every such call. Humanly speaking, they dared to be disloyal. Humanly speaking, they betrayed their country. Humanly speaking, they advocated courses that to the wisest seemed to lead to ruin. And if time has showed that they were *not* disloyal, but the truest patriots in Israel, that only means that in their word of prophecy they were moved by a wisdom higher than their own. They crushed into the dust their private prejudices. They shattered by their speech their private hopes. They flung to the winds, when they lifted up their voice, their private interests and advantages. And what I say is that if the word of prophecy had come to us solely by the will of man, the Bible would have a different tale to tell. No prophecy is of private interpretation. No one would dream it was who knows the prophets. It is not thus even the bravest speaks when he is speaking at the call of conscience. This is the speaking of men who in their darkness were under the moving of some mighty power that sat enthroned above the dust of things and saw the end from the beginning.

The same compulsion, as of some higher power, is seen in the portrayal of great Scripture characters. You have characters set up as an ideal, and then mysteriously that ideal is marred. The Jew had essentially a concrete mind. He loved to see all excellences embodied. He was at the heart of him a hero-worshiper, mightily influenced by old example. And that is one reason why in the Old Testament such a large place is given to biography in the lives of Abraham and of Moses and of David. Now remember that a Jewish writer never hesitated to idealize his hero.

If he thought it would tell for edification, he would paint a character without a flaw, unhesitatingly. And yet the strange thing is that in the Word of God these grand ideals which are to inspire the world are dashed with weakness, tarnished with iniquity, and broken sometimes by the most shameful fall. There was one hero who was the friend of God—what a glorious theme for any Jewish writer! There was another after God's own heart—can you not picture how he would be described? Yet the one—Abraham—descended to mean trickery, and the other—David—fell to the very depths. All this has been written down for us in the stern pages of the Word of God.

My friends, if the Scripture had come by the will of man, you would never have had anything of that. If prophecy had been a private rendering, you would have had lives like those of the medieval saints. And the very fact that you have falls like these in characters which were meant to lead the world is a witness to another will than ours. "When he, the Spirit of truth, is come," said Jesus, "he will guide you into all truth" (John 6:13). It was that Spirit which came upon the prophets and led them into the darkest truth unwillingly. Otherwise I cannot explain these tragic pages in writers who knew nothing of historic method, and who would never have hesitated to idealize the past for the glory of their people Israel.

And then, lastly, we trace the same compulsion in the self-revelation of the writers. We trace it in David in the fifty-first Psalm, for instance, and we have it manifestly in the apostles. I want you to remember that these apostolic writers were men of like passions with ourselves. They were actuated by the same desires, and they knew the pressure of our common hopes. They knew, as everyone must know, the desire to stand well with those who heard of them and to hand on to coming days some not unworthy memorial of themselves.

Now the point is that being men like that, they never hesitated to reveal themselves. They wrote of their weaknesses and of their sins in the very record that told the love of Christ. They concealed nothing for the sake of fame, sheltered nothing for the sake of honor, and cast no veil on an unworthy hour even in the sacred cause of friendship. Could not Peter have instructed Mark to cover up the tale of his denial? Might not John, being the friend of Peter, have dwelt a little less upon his fall? But the Scripture came not by the will of man, nor is any prophecy a private rendering. There it all stands written to this hour. There is no hurling of contempt at Judas—a chapter like *that* would have been very natural. There is no golden and enhaloed picture of the men who had left everything for Jesus. John knew not what spirit Christ was of. Peter denied Him with a fisher's curses. Judas, in a profound and awful silence, goes to his own place—and that is all. That is not the moving of the will; that is the moving of the Holy Spirit. *That* is the kind of thing which Scripture indicates when it says of itself it is inspired. If there be one thing growing ever clearer, as knowledge widens and the ages pass, it is that Scripture came not by the will of man.

Sound Doctrine or Healthy Teaching

Alexander Maclaren (1826–1910) was one of Great Britain's most famous preachers. While pastoring the Union Chapel, Manchester (1858–1903), he became known as "the prince of expository preachers." Rarely active in denominational or civic affairs, Maclaren invested his time in studying the Word in the original languages and sharing its truths with others in sermons that are still models of effective expository preaching. He published a number of books of sermons and climaxed his ministry by publishing his monumental *Expositions of Holy Scripture*.

This message was taken from *The Victor's Crowns*, published in 1902 by Funk and Wagnalls Company, New York.

Alexander Maclaren

9

SOUND DOCTRINE OR HEALTHY TEACHING

Hold fast the form of sound words, which thou hast heard of me, in faith and love which is in Christ Jesus (2 Timothy 1:13).

ANY GREAT AUTHOR or artist passes, in the course of his work, from one manner to another, so that a person familiar with him can date pretty accurately his books or pictures as being in his "earlier" or "later" style. So there is nothing surprising in the fact that there are great differences between Paul's last writings and his previous ones. The surprising thing would have been if there had not been such differences. The peculiarities of the so-called three pastoral Epistles (the two to Timothy and the one to Titus) are not greater than can fairly be accounted for by advancing years, changed circumstances, and the emergence of new difficulties and enemies.

Among them there are certain expressions that are very frequent in these letters and wholly unknown in any of Paul's other work. These have been pounced upon as disproving the genuineness of these letters. But they only do so if you assume that a man, when he gets old, must never use any words that he did not use when he was young, whatever new ideas may have come to him. Now in this text of mine is one of these phrases peculiar to these later letters—"sound words." That phrase and its parallel one, "sound doctrine," occur in all some half-dozen times in these letters and never anywhere else. The expression has become very common among us. It is more often used than understood. The popular interpretation of it hides its real meaning and obscures the very important lessons that are to be drawn from the true

127

understanding of it. Lessons that, I take leave to think, modern Christianity stands very sorely in need of. I desire now to try to unfold the thoughts and lessons contained in this phrase.

What Does Paul Mean by a "Form of Sound Words"?

I begin the answer by saying that he does not mean a doctrinal formula. The word here rendered "form" is the same which he employs in the first of the letters to Timothy when he speaks of himself and his own conversion as being "a pattern to them that should hereafter believe." The notion intended here is not a cut-and-dried creed, but a body of teaching that shall not be compressed within the limits of an iron form but shall be a pattern for the lives of the men to whom it is given. *The Revised Version* has "the pattern" and not "the form." I take leave to think that there were no creeds in the apostolic time and that the church would probably have had a firmer grasp of God's truth if there had never been any. At all events, the idea of a cast-iron creed, into which the whole magnificence of the Christian faith is crushed, is by no means Paul's idea in the word here.

Then, with regard to the other part of the phrase—"sound words"—we all know how that is generally understood by people. Words are supposed to be "sound" when they are in conformity with the creed of the critic. A sound High Churchman is an entirely different person from a sound Nonconformist. Puritan and Sacramentarian differ with regard to the standard that they set up, but they use the word in the same way to express theological statements in conformity with that standard. And we all know how harshly the judgment is sometimes made. We also know how easy it is to damn a man by a solemn shake of the head or a shrug of the shoulders and to question whether he is sound.

Now, all that is clean away from the apostolic notion of the word in question. If we turn to the other form of this phrase which occurs frequently in these letters, "sound doctrine," there is another remark to be made.

"Doctrine" conveys to the ordinary reader the notion of an abstract, dry, theological statement of some truth. Now, what the apostle means is not "doctrine" so much as "teaching." If you will substitute "teaching" for "doctrine," you will get much nearer to his thought just as you will get nearer it if for "sound," with its meaning of conformity to a theological standard, you substitute what the word really means—"healthy," wholesome, health-giving, healing. All these ideas run into each other. That which is in itself healthy is health-giving as food and as a medicine is healing. The apostle is not describing the teaching that he had given to Timothy by its conformity with any standard. But he is pointing to its essential nature as being wholesome and sound in a physical sense, and to its effect as being healthy and health-giving. Keep hold of that thought and the whole aspect of this saying changes at once.

There is only one other point that I would suggest in this first part of my sermon as to the apostolic meaning of these words. It is this: "healing" and "holy" are etymologically connected they tell us. The healing properties of the teaching to which Paul refers are to be found entirely in this: its tendency to make men better; to produce a purer morality, a loftier goodness, a more unselfish love; so to bring harmony and health into the diseased nature. The one healing for a man is to be holy. And, says Paul, the way to be holy is to keep a firm hold of that body of teaching that I have presented.

Now, that this tendency to produce nobler manners and purer conduct and holier character is the true meaning of the word "sound" here, and not "orthodox" as we generally take it, will be quite clear, I think, if you will notice how, in another part of these same letters, the apostle gives a long catalog of the things that are contrary to the health-giving doctrine. If the ordinary notion of the expression were correct, that catalog ought to be a list of heresies. But what is it? A black list of vices—"deceivers," "ungodly," "sinners," "unholy," "profane," "murderers," "manslayers," "whoremongers," "menstealers," "liars," "perjured" persons. Not one of these refers to aberration of opinion. All of them point to divergencies of conduct, and these are the things that are contrary to the healing doctrine. But they are not contrary, often, to sound orthodoxy. For there have been a great many imitators of that King of France, who carried little leaden images of saints and the Virgin in his hat and the Devil in his heart. "The form of sound words" is the pattern of healing teaching, which proves itself healing because it makes one holy. Now, that is my first question answered.

Where Paul Thought These Healing Words Were to Be Found

He had no doubt whatever as to that. They were in the message that he preached of Jesus Christ and His salvation. There and there only, in his estimation and inspired teaching, are such words to be found. The truth of Christ—His incarnation, His sacrifice, His resurrection, His ascension, the gift of His Divine Spirit—along with all the mighty truths on which these great facts rest and all which flow from these great facts, these, in the aggregate, are the health-giving words for the sickly world.

Now, historically, it is proved to be so. I do not need to defend, as if it were in full conformity with the dictates and principles of Christianity, the life and practice of any generation of Christian people. But this I do venture to say: that the world has been slowly lifted all through the generations by the influence—direct and indirect—of the great truths of Christianity. Today the very men who— in the name of certain large principles that they have learned from the Gospel—are desirous of brushing aside the old-fashioned Gospel are kicking down the ladder by which they climbed and that, with all the imperfections, for which we have to take shame to ourselves before God. Still the reflection of the perfect Image that is cast into the world from the mirror of the collective Christian conduct and character—though it be distorted by many a flaw in the glass and imperfect by reason of many a piece of the reflecting medium having dropped away—is still the fairest embodiment of character that the world has ever seen. Why, what is the meaning of the sarcasms that we have all heard until we are wearied of them, about "the Nonconformist conscience"? The adjective is wrong; it should be "the *Christian* conscience." But with that correction I claim the sarcasms as unconscious testimony to the fact that the Christian ideal of character and conduct set forth, and approximately realized, by religious people is far above the average morality of even a so-called Christian nation. And all that is due to the "pattern of health-giving words."

Now, the historical confirmation of Paul's claim that these health-giving words were to be found in his gospel is no more than is to be expected if we look at the contents of that Gospel to which he thus appeals. For there never has been such an instrument for regenerating individuals and society as lies in the truths of Christianity, firmly grasped and honestly worked out. Their healing power comes, first, from their giving the sense of pardon and acceptance. Friends, there is nothing, as I humbly venture to affirm, that will go down to the fountain and origin of all the ills of man except that teaching "God was in Christ reconciling the world to Himself, not imputing unto them their trespasses." That reality of guilt, that schism and alienation between man and God, must be dealt with first before you can produce high morality. Unless you deal with that central disease, you do very little. Something you do; but the cancer is deep-seated. The world's remedies for it may cure pimples on the surface, but they are powerless to extirpate the malignant tumor that has laid hold of the vitals. You must begin by dealing with the disease of sin—not only in its aspect as habit, but in its consequence of guilt and responsibility and separation from God—before you can bring health to the sick man.

And then, beyond that, I need but remind you of how a higher and more wholesome morality is made possible by these health-giving words. Inasmuch as they set forth for us the perfect example of Jesus Christ; inasmuch as they bring into operation love, the mightiest of all powers to mold a life; inasmuch as they open up for us, far more solemnly and certainly than ever else has been revealed, the solemn thought of judgment and of every man giving account of himself to God, and the assurance that "whatsoever a man soweth here, that"—a thousandfold increased in the crop—"shall he also reap in the eternities." In addition to the example of perfection in the beloved Christ—the mighty motive of love, the solemn urgency of judgment and retribution—the health-giving words bring to us the assurance of a Divine Power dwelling within us to lift us to heights of purity and goodness to which our unaided feet can never, never climb. And for all these reasons, the message of Christ's incarnation and death is the health-giving word for the world.

But, further, let me remind you that, according to the apostolic teaching, these healing and health-giving effects will not be produced except by that Gospel. Some of you, perhaps, may have listened to the first part of my sermon with approbation because it seemed to fit in with the general disparagement of doctrine prevalent in this day. Will you listen to this part, too? I venture to assert that although there are many men apart from Christ who have as clear a conception of what they ought to be and to do as any Christian, even aiming after high, pure, noble lives not altogether unsuccessfully, yet on the whole—on the wide scale and in the long run—if you change the "pattern of health-giving words," you lower the health of the world.

It seems to me that this generation is an object lesson in that matter. Why is it that these two things are running side by side in the literature of these closing years of the century—viz., a rejection of the plain laws of morality—especially in regard of the relations of the sexes—and a rejection of the old-fashioned Gospel of Jesus Christ? I venture to think that the two things stand to each other very largely in the relation of cause and effect. And if you want to bring back the world to Puritan morality, you will have to go back in the main to Puritan theology. I do not mean to insist upon any pinning of faith to any theological system. But this I am bound to say, and I beseech you to consider, that if you strike out from the "pattern of health-giving words"—the truth of the Incarnation, the sacrifice on the cross, the Resurrection, the Ascension, and the gift of the Spirit—what you have left are not enough to cure a fly.

What Paul Would Have Us Do with These "Health-Giving Words"

"Hold fast the form . . . in faith and love, which is in Christ Jesus." Now, that exhortation includes three things. Your time will not allow me to do more than just touch them. First it applies to the understanding. "Hold fast the teaching" by letting it occupy your minds. I am unwillingly bound to acknowledge my suspicion that a very large number of Christian people scarcely ever occupy their thoughts with the facts and principles of the Gospel, and that they have no firm and intelligent grasp of these, either singly or in their connection. I would plead for less newspaper and more Bible; for less novel and more Gospel. I know how hard it is for busy men to have spare energy for anything beyond their business and the necessary claims of society. But I would even venture to advise a little less of what is called Christian work in order to get a little more Christian knowledge. "Come ye yourselves apart into a solitary place," said the Master—and all busy workers need that. "Hold fast the health-giving words" by meditation, a lost art among so many Christians.

The exhortation applies next to the heart. "Hold . . . in faith and love." If that notion of the expression, which I have been trying to combat, were the correct one, there would be no need for anything beyond familiarizing the understanding with the bearings of the doctrinal truths. But Paul sees need for a great deal more. The understanding brings to the emotions that on which they fasten and feed. Faith—which is more than credence, being an act of the will—casts itself on the truth believed, or rather on the Person revealed in the truth; and love, kindled by faith and flowing out in grateful response and self-abandonment, are as needful as orthodox belief in order to hold fast the health-giving words.

The exhortation applies, finally, to character and conduct. Emotion, even when it takes the shape of faith and love, is as little the end of God's revelation as is knowledge. He makes Himself known to us in all the greatness of His grace and love in Jesus Christ, not that we may know, and there an end; nor even that knowing, we may feel, and there an end (though a great many emotional Christians seem to think that is all); but that knowing, we may feel, and knowing and feeling, we may be and do what He would have us do and be. We have the great river flowing past our doors. It is not only intended that we should fill our cisterns by knowledge, nor only bathe our parched lips by faith and love, but that we should use it to drive all the wheels of the mill of life. Not he that understands nor he that glows, but he that does is the man that holds fast the pattern of sound, health-giving words.

The world is like that five-porched pool in which were gathered a great multitude of sick folks. Its name is the "House of Mercy," for so Bethesda means, tragically as the title seems to be contradicted by the condition of the cripples and diseased lying there. But this fountain once moved gushes up forever, and whosoever will may step into it and immediately be made whole of whatsoever disease he has.

NOTES

Statutes and Songs

John Daniel Jones (1865–1942) served for forty years at the Richmond Hill Congregational Church in Bournemouth, England, where he ministered the Word with a remarkable consistency of quality and effectiveness, as his many volumes of published sermons attest. A leader in his denomination, he gave himself to church extension (he helped to start thirty new churches), assistance to needier congregations, and increased salaries for the clergy. He spoke at D. L. Moody's Northfield Conference in 1919.

This sermon was taken from *The Mundesley Bible Conference Report, 1916,* published by Morgan and Scott, London.

John Daniel Jones

10

STATUTES AND SONGS

Thy statutes have been my songs in the house of my pilgrimage (Psalm 119:54).

THERE IS NOT the slightest need to enter upon any critical discussion in order to appreciate the meaning and purpose of this psalm. It is a psalm in praise of the law of God. And the law of God that the psalmist has specially in mind is that which is expressed in the counsel, commands, and prohibitions of the Mosaic economy. He has varied names for that law—word, sayings, testimonies, judgment, statute, commandment, precept. But under all these differing names it is that law, which was the Hebrew boast and pride, that he is thinking of all the way through. In a score of ways he seeks to tell his readers how good and noble a thing the law is, and how he himself loves it and delights in it. But in all this long psalm he says nothing finer about the law than he says in my text, "Thy statutes have been my songs in the house of my pilgrimage."

Matthew Henry's comment upon this verse runs like this: "David was the sweet singer of Israel, and here we are told whence he fetched his songs: they were all borrowed from the Word of God. God's statutes were as familiar to him as the songs which men are accustomed to sing." Horace Bushnell, following in Matthew Henry's wake, pictures the Eastern traveler resting at midday from the heat or halting at some caravansary for the night, taking out his sackbut (the medieval and Renaissance trombone) or lyre and soothing his rest with a song of war or romance and love. But this psalmist finds his theme in the statutes of Jehovah. He sings not ballad of war or wine or love, but he sings of God's commandments and with them beguiles the weariness of the journey. "Thy statutes have been my song in the house of my pilgrimage."

Both Matthew Henry and Horace Bushnell are on the track of the psalmist's meaning, but their explanations fall short of the fullness of it. The psalmist means much more than that he found the words and themes for his songs in the statutes of the Lord. He means that the statutes inspired his songs. He means that the statutes themselves got converted into songs—that the commandments were to him like sweet music and that he enjoyed them and reveled in them as other people did in music and song. You remember how Wordsworth apostrophizes Duty, and what Duty was to Wordsworth the law was to this ancient singer. "Stern daughter of the voice of God" he calls Duty in one place and "Stern lawgiver" in another. "Stern"—there is something severe and almost menacing in the aspect of law. It sets men under restraint and imposes prohibitions upon them. But this psalmist has gotten far beyond the "Stern lawgiver" stage. Duty for him has become transfigured into delight. The harsh and peremptory notes of law have been transfigured into sweetest music. The burden has become a blessing. The demand has become a pleasure. The obligation has become a privilege. "Thy statutes have been my song in the house of my pilgrimage."

Now what I see in the contrast between Wordsworth and the psalmist is two stages of human experience, two levels of human attainment. At one stage duty is just the stern lawgiver, with an element of the harsh and forbidding about it. At the second and happier stage, the statutes become song and duty ceases to be harsh and forbidding and becomes a delight. And what I want to do for a few minutes this evening is to talk with you about these two stages and about the means by which we may pass from the one to the other. So here are my three divisions: first, the statute; second, the song; third, how the statute is changed into song.

The Statute

First of all, then, let me speak with you about the stage when the statute is a statute and nothing more, when duty is just the stern lawgiver, when law presents itself to us as a series of irksome and exacting precepts and prohibitions and demands. The apostle talks somewhere about the Jewish law being a schoolmaster to prepare the Jews for the teaching of Christ. It was meant to educate their moral and spiritual sense and so to fit them to receive Christ's larger and fuller revelation. Now that schoolmaster function belongs to all law. Its whole object is disciplinary and educative. Its prohibitions and demands are all meant to instruct men in moral distinctions, to educate their sense of right and wrong. And we—all of us—make the acquaintance of *law the schoolmaster*.

We make the acquaintance of law as soon as we wake to conscious life. Law makes its presence felt and known in our homes. Parents exercise authority over their children. The child discovers that he is not at liberty to do just what he likes. There are restraints and prohibitions on every hand. And not only is he not at liberty to do what he likes, but he is also often constrained to do what he does not like. His freedom is limited and curtailed in this direction and that. He is up against the primary and elementary moral statutes of which his parents are the exponents and administrators. And he discovers further that there is a certain compulsion and constraint behind the statute. Just exactly as the schoolmaster can punish idleness by detention and the cane, so the child discovers that disobedience to the statutes of the home brings punishment in the shape of penalty and pain. Our first experience of these statutes of the existence of law is in the home, and we find it irksome. As children we often fumed and fretted and rebelled against it.

As we grow older we find law elsewhere than in the home. We find law in *nature*. We find out there are certain things we may not and must not do. We discover that we must not play with fire or else we shall get burned. We discover that we must not lie down in the snow—although it seems to offer so soft a bed—or else we shall get frozen. Nature imposes new prohibitions upon us on this side and on that. She has her statutes that must be obeyed.

We find law in *society*. As soon as we wake up to the facts of social life, to the realization not simply that we are individuals but also members of a community, we find that community has defended itself by laws and statutes of various kinds. You cannot help yourself to anything you see that takes your fancy. There is a law against theft. You cannot go anywhere you please and turn in at any gate that offers a tempting prospect. There is a law against trespass. You cannot do exactly what you like on the public roads. You cannot drive your car or your bicycle at any speed you please. There is a law against furious driving. You cannot even say just what you think or speak just what you like. There is a law against libel. On every hand we find our liberty curtailed or limited. To many among us these statutes are burdensome and irksome. I have heard many a nature lover grumble against the law of trespass. I scarcely think a motorist exists who has not rebelled against the speed limits. These restraints chafe and gall men. But there they are, and behind them stand the policemen and the magistrate and the judge and the prison cell to enforce obedience.

And back of all these there is yet another law more stringent and exact than any—*the law of God,* which declares itself in conscience and reveals itself in the precepts and prohibitions, the counsels and demands of this old Book. All of us who are here this evening are under that law as well, and it is an infinitely more searching law than the law of society. We may wish we were not. But living as we do in this Christian land, instructed as we are in Christian truth, we cannot help ourselves. We cannot pretend that we do not know what the Lord requires of us. We know that He asks much more than that abstention from crime, which is all that the law of the land demands. We know that He expects us to do justly and to love mercy and to walk humbly with our God. We know that He expects us to keep ourselves unspotted from the world and to abstain from every appearance of evil. Many find these "statutes of the Lord"—the demands and prohibitions of the Christian life—intolerably burdensome. Many revolt against them. They want to know why their liberty should be limited, their pleasures curtailed, and their strongest impulses stifled.

The younger son left home because he could stand his father's statutes no longer. He wanted freedom for his impulses and lusts and passions. And so he made his journey into a far country. And many a youth rebels against God's statutes still. He sets conscience and this old Book at defiance. He thinks they interfere with the zest and fullness of life. He rejects and flouts the "statutes of the Lord" as forming a grievous and intolerable burden. And there are others of us who, while we do not perhaps rebel at the statutes or kick over the traces, find obedience to them more than a bit of a drudgery. Like the elder son in the parable, we do not transgress the commandment, but there is nothing glad or joyous in our obedience. We obey under constraint, and we often wish the statute were not there or that it could be relaxed. The tug of the world and the flesh is tremendous, and we have often wished that God's law was not quite so stringent and intolerant. We recognize that God's law is good, but we often feel that life would be easier and more enjoyable if it were not there. The statute is just a statute to us and nothing more, and obedience to it is burdensome and grievous.

The Song

Now, I want to pass on to say this: the statute fails of its intention if it remains a statute to the end of time. Law does not fulfill its function unless it educates us for something better than itself. Law is meant to educate us in our sense of right and wrong so that we may learn of our own impulse to shun the wrong and cleave to the right. Obedience, which at first is compelled and extorted by the statute, is meant to develop into obedience voluntarily and gladly given. There is really very little essential difference between disobedience and an obedience given under pressure and constraint. The man who is honest only because he is afraid of the law is at heart little better than the thief. The man who observes the conventional standard simply because he fears the consequences of a breach is, at heart, little better than the man who harbors lustful thoughts—although his outward life may be prim and respectable—and is really not much better than the open profligate, for he has already committed adultery in his heart.

The whole object of the discipline of the home and the statute law of life is to train us to love the right for its own sake. The real end of law is liberty, and so it is in the highest sphere of all. The law of God—as it declared itself in conscience and as it reveals itself in the precepts and commands of the Bible—fails of its purpose unless we learn to obey its behests, not because we fear the results of disobedience, but because we love what it commands —truth and honor and mercy and purity for their own sakes. Obedience has to become not compelled but spontaneous; not coerced, but willing and free. It must cease to become a drudgery and become a joy. Duty, the stern lawgiver, must for us as for Wordsworth change her aspect. We must begin to feel that "She wears the Godhead's most benignant grace; nor know we anything so fair, as the smile upon her face." The burden must become a boon. The constraint must be transformed into freedom. The demand must be changed into a delight. The statute must become a song.

Our Lord never meant us to remain at the stage in which duty is a drudgery. "Enter," He said, "into the joy of thy Lord." He meant us to share in the happy gladness of His own obedience. There was no constraint about our Lord's obedience to God. He obeyed because He delighted to obey. To do God's will was His pleasure. In the volume of the Book it was written of Him that He delighted to do God's will. Yes, God's law was within His heart. He sang a hymn even when God's will led Him to the bitter Cross. The statute for Christ had in very deed become a song. And Christ meant that same sort of joy to be in us. He meant our Christian service to be a glad, blithe, happy thing. There ought to be nothing doleful and dumpish and dismal about our lives—but a certain gaiety and irrepressible happiness. We ought to march to music; the statute ought to be converted into a song.

It often is so converted. You have—all of you—read J. M. Barrie's story of his mother, Margaret Ogilvy. It is a singularly touching and beautiful story of a son's devotion to his mother. Now I have no doubt that in Barrie's early days the duty of honoring his parents was instilled into him. That old command, "Honor thy father and mother," was pressed upon him. Obedience in his boyish days was a matter of statute, and sometimes—especially when it clashed with his pleasures—it may have been a bit irksome and burdensome. But when he became a man, and before he became a man, the statute had been converted into a song. To minister to that gentle, pale face was his purest joy. Not the smallest thing was left undone to make her happy. And all this ministry was no drudgery to him. There was nothing irksome or burdensome to him. It was glad, spontaneous, free. It was his supreme delight. It was his most fundamental pleasure. The statute had become a song.

I read the other day in the *Daily Telegraph* an article on France and the French soldier and the French people, which illustrates the very same thing. France is a military nation. She claims a right to the service of her sons. She says that when the need arises she has the right to ask her sons to risk limb and life on her behalf in battle. Military service in France is a matter of "Statute." But the men who are now fighting her battles have gotten far beyond the statute stage. Everyone who has visited France bears witness to the strangely exalted spirit that has taken possession of her people and that is making them almost rejoice in the cruel sacrifices they are compelled to make. The men in the trenches, the men who have been through the long-drawn agony of Verdun, are not fighting because they are compelled. They are not fighting for pay. They face that hell of suffering with something approaching ecstasy and rapture. "My love to my wife," cried one young officer as he fell, "my soul to God, and my life to France." The law asked for sacrifice, but there is no constraint about the sacrifices that the French are making. They are making them gladly, eagerly, exultingly. The statute has become a song.

In the same article, I read of an old French couple—man and wife, both over seventy—whose house was assigned to an English captain of artillery and his men as their billet. But it was no grudging hospitality these dear old folk gave the English stranger. The best the house could provide was set on the table for them. The best the house could do in the way of accommodation was placed at their disposal. In the course of the night the captain made a round of the place, and on the hard stone floor of an outhouse he found the old couple trying to rest. They had vacated their own little room that their English friends and allies might rest in a little more comfort. And when the captain brought them back into the house and chided them for exposing themselves to such hardships and risks, the old couple replied that it was nothing at all, that they rejoiced to do it for the friend of France. France asked of these old people a sacrifice. But the sacrifice had ceased to be a burden and had become a joy. The statute had been changed into a song.

There was a time when the statutes of the law were to the apostle Paul a burden too grievous to be borne. But later in his career, the commandments had ceased to be grievous. The service of Christ became perfect freedom to him. It entailed great and terrible hardships upon him. But Paul faced them all without moaning or complaint. He bore them with a certain eagerness and gladness. They flung him into prison, and he made the wall ring with the echoes of his songs at midnight. He counted it an honor that he was called upon to suffer for the Name. He was always rejoicing. He found deep and overmastering joy in speaking, working, and suffering for Christ. The statute had become a song.

I have been glancing, during this last week, through the diary of David Brainerd. How intense and devoted was that man's service! How he labored for his poor Indians! And how he suffered! The record of the last few months of his life is the record of what a flaming and eager spirit can do, even though the body is broken and the strength is spent. It was amid fevers and hemorrhages and the most absolute physical prostration that

David Brainerd did his work. But he rejoiced in it; he exulted in it. He did it with a kind of seraphic joy. Duty had become changed into a delight for him. The statute had become a song. And Brainerd names this as the fifth of the distinguishing marks of the Christian—the laws of God are his delight. He observes them not out of constraint or a servile fear of hell, but they are his choice. The strict observance of them is not his bondage, but his greatest liberty.

Tried by this test, how does our Christianity appear? What is the service of God to us? Is it a drudgery, or a delight? Do we find Christ's demands burdensome, or do we find His yoke to be easy and His burden light? Do we rejoice in our discipleship, or does it fret and chafe and gall us? Christ's service demands sacrifice. What about these sacrifices? Do we make them gladly? Do we find joy in them, or do they irritate and annoy us? Do we make them grudgingly? On what level are we—the level of the statute or the level of the song? Is it a case of stern duty, or do we delight to do God's will?

We are not real Christians until we reach this second stage. "The Lord is my strength and my song." Does the very thought of God make us sing? Do we find such joy in His service that life becomes musical? We are only slaves in the Father's house so long as our Christianity is just a matter of irksome drudgery. We become sons only when we delight to do the Father's will, and His statutes become our songs in the house of our pilgrimage—the source, that is, of our deepest and purest joys as we journey through this mortal life of ours.

How the Statute Is Changed Into Song

And now for just a minute or two I want to ask how it is the statute can be changed into a song, how duty can become transfigured into delight. There are two things I ought to say upon this head. I must say them very briefly. The first is this: The statutes themselves, as we practice them, reveal themselves to us not as harsh and irksome but as pleasant and delightful, so that insensibly, almost, our complaints and murmurings change into songs and thanksgivings. That is another great word of the psalmist's: "The statutes of the LORD are right, rejoicing the heart" (Ps. 19:8). The heart can never rejoice in the wrong. It can never be happy so long as we are on the wrong path. But the statutes of our Lord are *right*. The service to which He summons us is the one for which we were made. The duties He demands of us are in the deepest sense congenial. The heart is happy and at home in the doing of them. "The statutes of the LORD are right, rejoicing the heart." "Let him deny himself, and take up his cross daily, and follow me" (Luke 9:23). It sounds harsh and ugly and forbidding. But, strange enough, when we really try to obey, peace and joy come stealing into our souls. The statute becomes a song.

There is a verse in one of the historical books which says, "When the burnt offering began, the song of the LORD began also." When we do the difficult thing to which God summons, music begins to whisper in our souls. Men do not acquire the song by rejecting the statutes. You do not find joy and gladness among those who have repudiated God's law and cast away His cords from them. They do not sing in the far country. Disappointment and despair are at home there, but not joy and happiness. It is when men faithfully try to do God's will that the song begins. The harsh duty, when we tackle it, becomes a delight. You remember Tennyson's familiar lines:

> Not once or twice in our rough island story
> The path of duty was the way to glory;
> He that walks it, only thirsting for the right,
> And learns to deaden love of self,
> Before his journey closes,
> He shall find the stubborn thistle bursting
> Into glossy purples which outredden
> All voluptuous garden roses.

> Not once or twice in our rough island story
> The path of duty was the way to glory;
> He that ever following her commands
> On with toil of heart and knees and hands,
> Thro' the long gorge to the far light, has won

His path upward and prevailed,
Shall find the toppling crags of duty scaled,
Are close upon the shining tablelands,
To which our God is moon and sun.

God's demands, as we seek to discharge them, change themselves into delights. The statute naturally and inevitably, in the effort to obey, becomes a song.

But the second thing I have to say is this: Love is the great philosopher's stone that changes demand into delight, duty into joy, and statute into song. Love transmutes sacrifice into gladness. Think of our own lads this evening out in France. They are facing peril, wounds, death. In one sense you may say that they are under statute. When they enlisted they placed themselves under military law. But no law made them enlist. They volunteered. And it is not the statute now that makes them so willing and eager and enthusiastic. It is love of England that has accomplished that miracle. Love of England has converted sacrifice into a holy joy. It has transmuted the statute into a song.

Love makes every labor light. The seven years Jacob served for Rachel seemed but a few days for the love he had to her. "He's no heavy," said a little lassie, staggering along beneath the burden of a child almost as big as herself. "He's my brother." No man counts anything he does for his mother a burden. Love transmutes it into a privilege. It changes the statute to a song. And so it is in the highest sphere of all. It is love for Christ that is going to make His demands a delight and His service perfect freedom.

"Lovest thou Me?" said our Lord to Peter. He wanted to be sure upon that point before assigning him any duty. But when sure of the love, our Lord could say to him, "Feed My lambs. Feed My sheep." Without love the duty would have been sheer drudgery, irksome, distasteful, impossible. But with love in the heart, the duty would become a delight, and the statute a song. That was the secret of Paul's enthusiasm and gladness and exuberant joy. That was what enabled him to rejoice ever amid all his sorrows. His heart was full of love for Christ who died.

And it is love that will transport us out of the bleak and dreary land of drudgery into the land of delight, and that will make our Christian service happy and glad and exultant. It is because we love Christ so little that sometimes we feel His commandments to be grievous. It is more love we want in order to transfigure everything for us. And the place to get that more love is at His Cross. My friends, when we love Christ better, the duties and sacrifices He asks of us will just become sources of joy and gladness. His statutes will become our songs in the house of our pilgrimage.

NOTES

What the Bible Demands If We Are to Understand It

William Culbertson (1905–1971) was born and educated in Philadelphia and was identified all of his ministry with the Reformed Episcopal Church of America. He pastored churches in Pennsylvania and New Jersey and in 1937 was elected Bishop of the New York and Philadelphia Synod. In 1942, he became Dean of Education at the Moody Bible Institute in Chicago; and in 1947 was named acting president upon the death of Will H. Houghton. In 1948, he became president of the school, a position he held with distinction until 1971, when he was named Chancellor. "My first impression and the lasting one," said Dr. Wilbur M. Smith, "is that he is a man of God." He was in great demand as a preacher and widely recognized as a leader in Christian education.

This sermon comes from the compilation of his Moody Bible Institute "Founder's Week" messages, *The Faith Once Delivered,* published in 1972 by Moody Press, and is used by permission.

William Culbertson

11

WHAT THE BIBLE DEMANDS IF WE ARE TO UNDERSTAND IT

We speak God's wisdom in a mystery, even the wisdom that hath been hidden, which God foreordained before the worlds unto our glory: which none of the rulers of this world hath known: for had they known it, they would not have crucified the Lord of glory: but as it is written,

Things which eye saw not, and ear heard not,
And which entered not into the heart of man,
Whatsoever things God prepared for them
that love him.

But unto us God revealed them through the Spirit: for the Spirit searcheth all things, yea, the deep things of God. For who among men knoweth the things of a man, save the spirit of the man, which is in him? even so the things of God none knoweth, save the Spirit of God. But we received, not the spirit of the world, but the spirit which is from God; that we might know the things that were freely given to us of God (1 Corinthians 2:7–12 ASV).

I SHOULD LIKE to speak to you on the theme, "What the Bible demands if we are to understand it." A text, which brings such a subject before us, has been on my mind and heart for some time. It is from the eighth chapter of Acts and is the story of Philip and the Ethiopian eunuch. "Philip ran to him, and heard him reading Isaiah the prophet, and said, Understandeth thou what thou readest? And he said, How can I?" (vv. 30–31). It is the answer to that question, "How can I?" to which I propose to direct our attention this morning.

At the outset, let me say that I am not suggesting that it is possible to comprehend fully all that is in the Word of God. With the psalmist I confess, "How great are thy works, O Jehovah! Thy thoughts are very deep" (Ps. 92:5). But I would remind you that it is possible to have some understanding of the Word, and I would observe that for most of us it should be greater than it is.

But I have another matter on my heart, which I believe the Lord wants me to speak of today. There is a good deal being said, written, and done that makes out as though the Bible were merely a human book that can be understood and explained merely by human investigation. The article in "the double issue" of *Life* for December 25, 1964, is for the most part notorious in this respect. The same idea seems inherent in the attempt by scholars, widely differing in faith, to formulate a common version for all these faiths. This project seems to say that a translation is merely a mechanical procedure. All you need is a group of scholars who have the knowledge and vocabulary, grammar, history, and some sympathy with the general import of what is said in the Scriptures. But what does the Bible itself say? What are the requirements that it demands? Thank God for scholars who have given us the Word of God in our own language. We do not make light of this gift. But we still insist that the Bible has some requirements that even scholars must meet if they are to understand God's Word. It will do us all good to look at these demands.

The Bible has its stipulations. Not just anybody can understand it. That everybody cannot understand the Bible is not because it is mystical, esoteric, or cryptic. It is not because it is necessary to look for hidden meanings. It is not because it contains irrational statements, although there are mysteries beyond our comprehension. Infinite revelation to finite minds is bound to present difficulties. But an understanding of what may even be termed the elementary teaching of the Word of God is denied those who fail to meet the Bible's demands. What are they? Let us list some of them.

Salvation

With the understanding that there will be some overlapping, there are broadly at least five such stipulations the Word of God makes for its own understanding. The first of these is the necessity of *salvation*. By salvation,

I mean a salvation which involves the new birth. The Lord Jesus said to Nicodemus, "Verily, verily, I say unto thee, Except one be born anew, he cannot see the kingdom of God" (John 3:3). At this point the Lord Jesus did not say he cannot *enter* the kingdom of God. He said that later in verse 5. But in verse 3 He declares the kingdom of God cannot even be *seen* unless a man is born anew. "Now the natural man receiveth not the things of the Spirit of God: for they are foolishness unto him; and he cannot know them, because they are spiritually judged" (1 Cor. 2:14). A man not knowing what it means to be saved, not having been born again, is by the Bible's own definition incapable of understanding its revelation, for he doesn't understand the things of the Spirit of God. The apostle Paul in Romans 8:6–7 lays down the principle: "The mind of the flesh is death; but the mind of the Spirit is life and peace: because the mind of the flesh is enmity against God; for it is not subject to the law of God, neither indeed can it be."

The utter impossibility of that which is flesh understanding that which is spirit is, it seems to me, fully demonstrated in these quotations from the Word of God.

Now, in this matter of salvation, faith is an inherent part—faith in the Savior. I trust that those hearing my voice this morning have long since made a decision to turn from their sins to the Savior, that you know what it means to be a child of God—not by the world's definition of the term, but by the biblical definition. "As many as received him, to them gave he the right to become children of God, even to them that believe on his name" (John 1:12).

There is no shortcut; there is no way around. Salvation is necessary to enter into the meaning of the Word of God. Faith, then, is involved in this transaction—faith placed in the Son of God who died and rose again that men might be saved.

Faith that God has spoken is also involved. The God who spoke through the prophets has "at the end of these days spoken unto us in his Son" (Heb. 1:1–2). There is a revelation. The Bible claims to be that revelation. It claims to have been brought to us by holy men who were moved by the Holy Spirit. It claims that it is the product of inspiration, the inspiration of God. "Thus saith the Lord" occurs again and again on its pages. So we believe that God has spoken.

By faith I do not mean, as is sometimes proposed, a leap in the dark. Faith can be rationally satisfying. For when we posit the God of the Scriptures, the possibility of divine revelation is established. Furthermore, from that vantage point, the whole revelation of what God says concerning God, man, sin, and eternity ties together and makes exquisite sense. Granted, there are mysteries, and we get beyond our depth. But there is no questioning the great essentials of our faith.

Involved also in this necessity for salvation to understand the Word of God is what the Bible speaks of as the creation of the new man. "Put on the new man, that after God hath been created in righteousness and holiness of truth" (Eph. 4:24). That new man created by God has the capacity to understand God as we are taught by the Spirit of God.

Salvation is absolutely necessary to understand the Word of God. May I simply observe, how can men who make light of the Gospel—the necessity of the shed blood of our Lord, the reality of His resurrection—have faith in the Savior? Therefore what they say contrary to the Scriptures should not influence one who knows God in salvation.

Simplicity

In the second place, the Bible itself makes as one of its demands, if it is to be understood, that the individual who opens its pages and pores over its message be characterized by *simplicity*. By simplicity I mean plainness, I mean artlessness, I mean humility, I mean unsophistication. I do not mean foolishness.

Listen to the Lord Jesus: "Verily I say unto you, Whosoever shall not receive the kingdom of God as a little child, he shall in no wise enter therein" (Mark 10:15).

In Matthew 11, immediately after our Lord has denounced certain cities that were given the inestimable privilege of hearing the Son of God Himself speak to them—Chorazin, Bethsaida, and Capernaum—we find that "at that season" (when in their sophistication, when in their worldly wiseness, when in their living wholly for the present) they turned away from the message of the Son of God. "Jesus answered and said, I thank thee, O Father, Lord of heaven and earth, that thou didst hide these things from the wise and understanding, and didst reveal them unto babes: yea, Father, for so it was well-pleasing in thy sight" (vv. 25–26). And that is still true.

In the recent issue of *Life* to which I have made reference, there is a quotation from a great scholar, Rudolf Bultmann: "I do indeed think that we can now know almost nothing concerning the life and personality of Jesus." On another page, a caption reads, "John's version is a puzzle to scholars." Strange indeed. I have known humble, unlettered souls whose lives have been transformed because they knew Him. I say no more. He has hidden these things from the wise and from the understanding, and has revealed them to babes. Unless we approach Him in simplicity of heart, we shall forever remain in ignorance of Him and of what He can do.

Spirituality

The Bible's third demand, if it is to be understood, is the need for *spirituality*. First Corinthians 2, I think, makes this abundantly plain. "Things which eye saw not, and ear heard not, and which entered not into the heart of man, whatsoever things God prepared for them that love him" (v. 9).

Incidentally, that doesn't mean what a lot of people think it means. They think it has reference only to the things of eternity, which we will discover when we shuffle off this mortal coil and go to heaven. That's not what it means. The emphasis is on things that entered not into the heart of *man*, things that *man* cannot discover, things that *man* cannot study out, things that *man* of himself cannot comprehend. The things you don't know as a man, you know as a *born-again man*. That is the emphasis.

Notice, "Unto us God revealed them through the Spirit: for the Spirit searcheth all things, yea, the deep things of God" (v. 10).

The Spirit of God is not ours by virtue of our birth into the human family. Jude 19, a passage dealing with apostates, reads: "These are . . . sensual." The word "sensual" is exactly the same word translated "natural" in 1 Corinthians 2:14. The natural man cannot understand the things of the Spirit. He is limited to the things of time and space, and is devoid of knowledge of the Spirit. He is earthbound. He is natural, not having the Spirit. And so I observe that the Spirit of God is not ours naturally.

In the second place, the Spirit of God is given to those who obey: "the Holy Spirit, whom God hath given to them that obey him" (Acts 5:32). And when in obedience to the Gospel we turn from our sin and place our faith in the Savior who loved us, who died for us, who rose again, not only are we saved, but part of that salvation is the gift of the Holy Spirit.

In the third place, *all* believers have the Spirit of God. "If any man hath not the Spirit of Christ, he is none of his" (Rom. 8:9). "Know ye not that your body is a temple of the Holy Spirit which is in you, which ye have from God?" (1 Cor. 6:19). And I remind you that this word was spoken to believers, even carnal believers. "Because ye are sons, God sent forth the Spirit of his Son into our hearts, crying Abba, Father" (Gal. 4:6). All believers have the Spirit of God.

Fourth, the Holy Spirit is the great Illuminator of the revelation of God. Having given the revelation through holy men, He becomes the Illuminator of that revelation: "Ye need not that any one teach you; but as his anointing teacheth you concerning all things, and is true, and is no lie, and even as it taught you, ye abide in him" (1 John 2:27).

The anointing that we receive is the Spirit of God. He is the great Teacher. The conclusion I wish to reach in this matter is simply this: If we are to understand the Word of God, we shall have to be taught by the Spirit. The Holy Spirit is the Illuminator of the divine revelation. So there must be an adjustment to the Spirit of God if we are to understand the Word of God. We must have Him, and we must be spiritual. Said the apostle to the Corinthian Christians, "I . . . could not speak unto you as unto spiritual, but as unto carnal, as unto babes in Christ" (1 Cor. 3:1). May I remind you that the first two syllables of the word "spiritual" are "spirit," and that is indicative of the fact that the Holy Spirit is essential and is central in all true spirituality. He, unhindered, unrestrained, must have the right of reign in our hearts if He is to exercise His function as Teacher. Then the Word of God will be open to our wondering view. Do you have these—salvation, simplicity, spirituality?

Study

Fourth is the necessity for *study*. I read in the Book of God the motto of Moody Bible Institute: "Study to shew thyself approved unto God, a workman that needeth not to be ashamed, rightly dividing the word of truth" (2 Tim. 2:15 KJV).

For though the Holy Spirit is the Teacher, and I make much of this truth, the fact of the matter is that He teaches us from the Book. Study, rightly divide. "Handling aright the word of truth," says the *American Standard Version*. What is that word concerning the righteous man in Psalm 1? It is this: "His delight is in the law of Jehovah; and on his law doth he meditate day and night" (v. 2). What was the word from Deuteronomy that the Lord used to repel Satan in the wilderness? "Man shall not live by bread alone, but by every word that proceedeth out of the mouth of God" (Matt. 4:4).

I remember a quaint sentence in George Henderson's little book, *Exodus:* "The Bible is unlike any other book, in that one must personally know its Author before one can really understand its contents; it resembles other books in that to be understood it must be read; to be known it must be studied." There is no shortcut to an understanding of the revelation of God.

I would remind you that it is in this Book that God has revealed Himself and His will. We need this Book to correct our erroneous concepts and our partial insights into truth.

> To the law and to the testimony! If they speak not according to this word, surely there is no morning for them (Isa. 8:20).

> He that rejecteth me, and receiveth not my sayings, hath one that judgeth him: the word that I spake, the same shall judge him in the last day (John 12:48).

> If any man thinketh himself to be a prophet, or spiritual, let him take knowledge of the things which I write unto you, that they are the commandment of the Lord. But if any man is ignorant, let him be ignorant (1 Cor. 14:37–38).

May I once again emphasize, perhaps unnecessarily for some, this matter of the humanistic approach to the Word of God, and the approach to the Word of God of one who believes in the supernatural. These are two opposite, entirely contradictory, and utterly opposing concepts. Actually, in this matter of whether the Bible is a divine revelation or whether it is man's quest for religious truth is the basic difference between the liberal and the fundamentalist. To the Bible believer, the Bible is inspired by God, and it is indeed the truth of God's message for man. It is God's revelation of Himself, of man, of this world, and the next. But, to the liberal, the Bible is largely, if not altogether, man's quest for religious truth. We as evangelicals recognize that God spoke through holy men—God used men. The modernist's approach is that the Bible is merely a human record. The conservative accepts the testimony of the Book and of the Lord of the Book. "Men spake from God, being moved by the Holy Spirit" (2 Peter 1:21). "The scripture cannot be broken" (John 10:35). We must study that revelation. It is not something that we invent. It is not something that comes out of a capacity of natural man either to invent or to understand. It is a revelation from God. The Word of God understood, believed, and obeyed means a life of joy and peace.

Subjection

There is a fifth necessity, the necessity for *subjection,* submissiveness to God. It is not without meaning that in that tremendous chapter on yieldedness, on the appropriation of Christ as our life—Romans 6—that a passage is devoted to the theme of obedience:

> Thanks be to God, that, whereas ye were servants of sin, ye became obedient from the heart to that form of teaching where unto ye were delivered; and being made free from sin, ye became servants of righteousness. I speak after the manner of men because of the infirmity of your flesh: for as ye presented your members as servants to uncleanness and to iniquity unto iniquity, even so now present your members as servants to righteousness unto sanctification. For when ye were servants of sin, ye were free in regard of righteousness. What fruit then had ye at that time in the things whereof ye are now ashamed? For the end of those things is death. But now being made free from sin and become servants to God, ye have your fruit unto sanctification, and the end eternal life (vv. 17–22).

Notice in verse 22, you became "servants to God"—or according to the margin, "bondservants." And so I go back to verse 16: "Know ye not, that to whom ye present yourselves as servants unto obedience, his servants ye are whom ye obey; whether of sin unto death, or of obedience unto righteousness." Willful disobedience to the known will of God will block your understanding of the revelation of God.

There were believers who chose to remain in carnality instead of going on with God. And what is carnality? Indulgence in the things of time and sense which rule out our out-and-out dedication to God. And a word had to be spoken to them: "When by reason of the time ye ought to be teachers, ye have need again that some one teach you the rudiments of the first principles of the oracles of God; and are become such as have need of milk, and not of solid food" (Heb. 5:12).

Remember a parallel passage in 1 Corinthians 3 and understand that milk is the food of one who has not gone on with God, one who has been born again but has remained in infancy because other things occupy his attention and his heart. "Everyone that partaketh of milk is without experience of the word of righteousness." The thing God is driving at is not merely a theoretical comprehension of the revelation—it is an experiential realization in life of the meaning of that revelation. And unsubmissiveness and unyieldedness block the pathway to that which God is after—to conform you to the image of His Son.

And so here are five demands that I believe the Lord makes if we are to understand what He wants us to understand in the Book of God: *salvation, simplicity, spirituality, study,* and *subjection.* Humble believers and learned scholars may know the Lord and the Book if they meet the conditions. Remember, the Bible makes its own demands as to who may understand it.

At Moody Bible Institute we love the Bible. We love the Lord of the Bible. And, God helping us, we will remain true to the great fact that the Bible in the original autograph was the inspired, inerrant, infallible Word of the living God.